Workbook/Laboratory Manual
(Part A)
to accompany

YOOKOSO!

Workbook/Laboratory Manual
(Part A)
to accompany

YOOKOSO!
An Invitation to Contemporary Japanese

よ う こ そ

Sachiko Fuji

Hifumi Ito
University of California, San Diego

Hiroko Kataoka
University of Oregon

Yumiko Shiotani
University of Oregon

Yasu-Hiko Tohsaku
University of California, San Diego

McGraw-Hill. Inc.

New York   St. Louis   San Francisco   Auckland   Bogotá   Caracas   Lisbon
London   Madrid   Mexico City   Milan   Montreal   New Delhi   San Juan
Singapore   Sydney   Tokyo   Toronto

This is an book.

This book is printed on recycled paper containing
10%post consumer waste.

Workbook/Laboratory Manual, Part A, to accompany
Yookoso! An Invitation to Contemporary Japanese

Copyright © 1994 by McGraw-Hill, Inc. All rights reserved. Printed in the United States of America.
Except as permitted under the United States Copyright Act of 1976, no part of this publication may be
reproduced or distributed in any form or by any means, or stored in a data base or retrieval system,
without the prior written permission of the publisher.

3 4 5 6 7 8 9 0 MAL MAL 9 0 0 8 7 6 5 4

ISBN: 0-07-072293-5

The compositors were Mitaka and GTS Graphics.
The development editor was Karen Sandness and the editing supervisor was Christina Dekker.
The production supervisor was Tanya Nigh.
Illustrations were provided by Rick Hackney.
Production assistance was provided by Tulip Graphics.
Malloy Lithographing, Inc., was printer and binder.

Table of Contents

To the Instructor

This *Workbook/Laboratory Manual A* and *Workbook/Laboratory Manual B* are designed to accompany *Yookoso!: An Invitation to Contemporary Japanese*.

They offer a variety of listening and writing exercises to reinforce the vocabulary and structures presented in the main text, along with explanations, charts, and exercises for the newly introduced **hiragana**, **katakana**, and **kanji**. Part A contains the exercises for *Getting Started*, Chapters One through Three and Review Chapter One, while Part B contains the exercises for Chapters Four through Seven and Review Chapter Two.

Each chapter consists of three sections: *Listening Comprehension Activities*, *Kanji Exercises*, and *Writing Activities*. The *Writing Exercises* section of *Getting Started* offers **hiragana** and **katakana** exercises, while the *Kanji Exercises* in Chapters One through Seven provide exercises for the active **kanji** presented in the main text. In *Getting Started*, the *Listening Comprehension Activities* and *Writing Activities* are all written in romanization, but in the subsequent chapters, they are written in **hiragana**, **katakana**, and **kanji**. Only those **kanji** previously presented for active mastery are used, so no **hurigana** are provided anywhere in the *Workbook/Laboratory Manual*. We recommend, therefore, that students finish the *Kanji Exercises* before doing the *Writing Activities*.

The *Listening Comprehension Activities* and *Writing Activities* for each chapter are divided into topical subsections corresponding to those in the main textbook. After completing a given subsection in the main textbook, the instructor can assign the appropriate exercises in the *Workbook/Laboratory Manual*.

In the *Listening Comprehension Activities*, we have made every effort to provide the students with authentic-sounding Japanese discourse, in both dialogues and monologues, but the questions and instructions are given in English, so that the student can concentrate fully on the content of the recorded material without spending a lot of time decoding written Japanese. All the spoken material for the *Listening Comprehension Activities* is recorded in the tape program, and the tape scripts are included in the *Instructor's Manual*.

The *Kanji Exercises* section consists of two parts. The first is a chart of the active **kanji** presented in each chapter, and the second presents exercises for both reading and writing those **kanji**.

In the *Writing Activities* section, the exercises progress from mechanical exercises to those requiring dialogue completion or creative or personalized responses. Several creative activities are based on realia or authentic materials. Any of these exercises may be done as group or pair activities in class or individually at home. In addition to topic- or function-based exercises, some chapters include opportunities for practicing specific grammatical structures presented in the *Grammar Notes* of the main text.

The *Review Chapters* are designed like those in the main text, so that students can review previously learned vocabulary and structures in an integrated way.

In addition to the cast of characters from the main text, a separate set of characters appears throughout the *Workbook/Laboratory Manual*. Most of these are students of Japanese at an American university and their Japanese-speaking acquaintances. This is because of the authors' belief that any instructional program for learners studying Japanese outside of Japan must provide them with the vocabulary and skills necessary for talking about their own lives.

The answers to all the exercises are included in the *Instructor's Manual*. The authors would like to express their sincere appreciation to Thalia Dorwick, Foreign Language Publisher at McGraw-Hill, Inc., for her guidance, suggestions, and insightful comments on the development of this *Workbook/Laboratory Manual*. We are also deeply indebted to Karen Sandness for her superb editing. Finally, we must note the invaluable assistance of the capable production staff at McGraw-Hill, Inc.

Sachiko Fuji
Hifumi Ito
Hiroko Kataoka
Yumiko Shiotani
Yasu-Hiko Tohsaku

To the Student

The format of *Workbook / Laboratory Manual A* and *Workbook / Laboratory Manual B* follows that of the main textbook: Part A contains the exercises for *Getting Started*, Chapters One through Three and Review Chapter One, while B contains the exercises for Chapters Four through Seven and Review Chapter Two.

Each of the main chapters consists of three sections.

Listening Comprehension Activities
Kanji Exercises
Writing Activities

Getting Started has *Hiragana/Katakana Exercises* instead of *Kanji Exercises*.

The *Listening Comprehension Activities* section contains questions and activities based on the dialogues and narratives recorded in the accompanying tape program. These recordings provide you with opportunities to listen to spoken Japanese in a variety of contexts and to practice and test your listening skills outside the classroom.

The listening comprehension activities include open-ended, multiple choice, or true-false questions and fill-in-the-blank exercises for you to work on while listening to the tape. The written instructions explain the task and provide you with a general idea of the context and the speakers of the dialogues or narratives. In some cases, further instructions tell you how many times you should listen to the tape while answering the questions. All instructions and questions are given in English, so that you can practice listening to spoken Japanese without worrying about understanding written Japanese.

We suggest that you follow these steps when you do the *Listening Comprehension Activities*:

1. Read the instructions carefully so that you understand the topic and context of the recording and who the speakers are. If possible, guess what vocabulary might be used and figure out how much of it you already know in Japanese.
2. Study any new vocabulary that is provided after the instructions.
3. Before reading the questions in the tasks, listen to the recording once. Think about whether or not you have understood the gist of the passage and how much specific information you have been able to comprehend.
4. Read through the questions. Figure out what information you need to answer them.
5. Listen to the recording again, concentrating on finding the information you need.
6. Unless otherwise specified in the instructions, listen to the recording as many times as necessary. Do not, however, stop the recording in the middle of the dialogues or narratives. (In real-life situations, no one will stop talking for your convenience while you are eavesdropping.) If necessary, review the vocabulary, expressions, and structures in the corresponding sections of the main textbook before repeating this process.

In most of the listening activities, you can answer the questions without understanding everything in the recording. Even when listening to spoken English in everyday life you can often get the gist of a conversation or the specific information you want without understanding every single word. You will find that the same strategy works for Japanese.

One effective way to develop your listening skills is to listen to your Japanese tapes as much as possible. You can listen to them while exercising, doing household chores, riding public transportation, or just relaxing. Or, you can listen to the tapes in the car while driving around town or while stuck in traffic. At any rate, try to pay attention to the general content of the recordings. You will find that the more you listen to the tapes, the more you will understand and the better your listening skills will become.

You can also use the tapes for improving your pronunciation. After you are able to comprehend the gist of a recorded segment, pay attention to the speakers' intonation and rhythm. Try to repeat after them and mimic them.

It is natural for beginning students to speak Japanese with the accent of their native language. Worrying too much about pronunciation can slow down your speech production or even make you too self-conscious to communicate effectively. On the other hand, severe pronunciation problems can prevent people from understanding you or lead to embarrassing mistakes: You will need to work on any such problems that your instructor points out. On the whole, however, native speakers are more interested in the content of your speech than in your pronunciation.

The *Hiragana/Katakana Exercises* and the *Kanji Exercises* sections are designed to provide you with practice in writing **hiragana**, **katakana**, and the active **kanji** presented in the main chapters of the textbook. Each section consists of charts on the meanings, readings, and stroke order of each character, followed by exercises. The **hiragana/katakana** charts are self-explanatory, and the **kanji** charts are organized in the following way:

Kanji charts

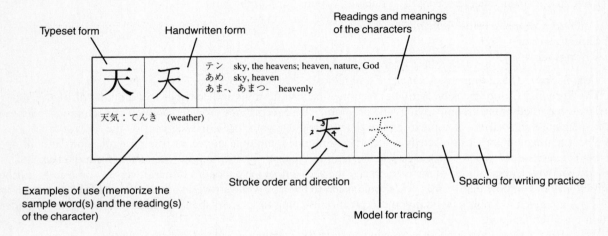

The Latin alphabet has no set stroke-order, so many English-speaking students tend to ignore the rules for writing **kanji** and develop bad habits that result in misshapen characters. You must follow the set stroke-order and direction. Your characters will look better, and practicing the correct way of writing will help imprint the shape of the character in your memory. The chart has only two spaces for practicing each character so for additional practice use engineering graph paper. Best of all is the special "**kanji**-ruled" paper, called **genkooyooshi** in Japanese, that can often be found in Japanese or Chinese import stores.

It is always a good idea to learn a new **kanji** along with its most commonly occurring compounds or with its **okurigana** (**hiragana** endings) instead of as an isolated symbol. For this reason we have provided exercises in which you either write the pronunciation of a **kanji** or compound in **hiragana** or insert **kanji** into sentences. The more you see and write the new **kanji** in meaningful contexts, the better you will remember them.

The *Writing Activities* give you the opportunity to use the vocabulary, expressions, and structures presented in the main text in their written forms as you practice expressing your ideas and thoughts in Japanese. Like the *Listening Comprehension Activities*, the *Writing Activities* are divided into the same topical subsections as the main textbook, so refer to the relevant sections if you have any questions. Only **kanji** presented before or in the current chapter are used in the *Writing Activities*. We recommend that you go over the *Kanji Exercises* section first. Then the *Writing Activities* will provide extra reinforcement for the **kanji** you have just learned.

In addition to the cast of characters from the main text, a separate set of characters appears throughout the *Workbook/Laboratory Manual*. The first group of characters is Professor Arai, a Japanese language professor at a North American university, and her students from various countries: Cody Smith, Antonio Coronado, Lois Johnson, Peggy Yu, Jin Mi Kim, Hans Kraus, and Ryan Scott. These students use Japanese in their language class and as a means of communication with the second group of characters, who are their Japanese-speaking friends or roommates: Midori Momoi, Kunio Satoo, and Maria Nakajima. The third set of characters is Masaru Honda, a Japanese television interviewer, and Himiko, a popular and extravagantly eccentric singer and actress. Honda conducts a series of interviews with Himiko throughout the *Workbook/Laboratory Manual*.

As you hear and read about these characters, you will learn to talk and write about your own life and concerns as an English-speaking student of Japanese.

GETTING STARTED
PART ONE

Listening Comprehension Activities

Meeting Others and Introducing Yourself

Listen as Kunio Satoo looks for Smith from Bank of America among the people present at a party, and then complete the following summary, using the words or phrases listed below. Each item is used once.

Satoo says _____ when he approaches a person for the first time and _____

when he finds out it is not the right person. Smith says _____ to affirm that he is indeed the

person Satoo is looking for. Satoo and Smith exchange _____ in order to introduce

themselves. Satoo and Smith greet each other by saying _____.

1. meeshi   2. shitsuree shimashita   3. hajimemashite   4. soo desu   5. sumimasen

Everyday Greetings

Listen to the following three dialogues and choose the words from the list below that describe the situations being portrayed. You may find more than one description for each situation, and some descriptions may be used more than once.

1. _____   2. _____   3. _____

a. morning   b. any time of the day   c. afternoon   d. meeting before leaving   e. meeting for the first time
f. meeting after a long time

Asking What Something Is

A. Listen as Professor Arai's students learn the names of classroom objects. Then circle the items mentioned in the conversation.

table	ceiling
chalk	window
textbook	desk
door	chair

B. A Japanese traveling in the United States wants to try American cuisine. He visits a cafeteria with a friend who has lived in the States for several years and asks questions about the food. Answer the questions at the end of each of the four exchanges by circling either hai (yes) or iie (no).

1. hai/iie   2. hai/iie   3. hai/iie   4. hai/iie

Writing Activities

Meeting Others and Introducing Yourself

A. A stranger approaches you on the street, looking for someone he or she has never met. Write your half of the conversation. Be sure that what you write makes sense when taken together with what the stranger says.

STRANGER: Sumimasen, Kawamura-san desu ka.

   YOU: _____ 1

STRANGER: Shitsuree shimashita.

   YOU: _____ 2

B. You are looking for Mr. Hayashi, whom you have never met, in front of a station. Complete the following dialogue.

   YOU: _____ 1

STRANGER: Iie.

   YOU: _____ 2

STRANGER: Iie.

C. Choose the most appropriate response from the right column.

1. _____ Sumimasen, Hayashi-san desu ka.
2. _____ Onamae wa?
3. _____ Hajimemashite.
4. _____ Doozo yoroshiku.

   a. Chin desu.
   b. Hajimemashite.
   c. Doozo yoroshiku.
   d. Iie.

D. What would you say in the following situations? Choose your answers from the options given below.

1. _____ You are meeting someone for the first time.
2. _____ You want to know someone's name.
3. _____ You are introducing yourself and stating your professional affiliation.
4. _____ You are handing over your name card.
5. _____ Someone has given you his/her name card.
6. _____ You have finished introducing yourself.

   a. Doozo yoroshiku.
   b. Arigatoo gozaimasu.
   c. Sonii no Takada desu.
   d. Kore, watashi no meeshi desu.
   e. Hajimemashite.
   f. Onamae wa?

E. Write dialogues for the following situations, following the cues provided. Do not translate the cues. Just use them as general guidelines for the conversations.

1. Kawamura and Ms. Tanaka meet each other for the first time.

Kawamura meets Tanaka for the first time. He greets her.   K: _____ 1

Tanaka returns the greeting.   T: _____ 2

Kawamura says that he is Kawamura of the University of Tokyo.

K: _____ 3

Then he hands Tanaka his name card as he says, "Nice to meet you."

_____ 4

Tanaka thanks Kawamura and hands him her card as she says that she is Tanaka from Keio University and that she is glad to meet him.

T: _____ 5

_____ 6

_____ 7

Kawamura thanks Tanaka.

K: _____ 8

2. Kawamura is supposed to meet Mr. Yamashita for the first time at a nearby train station.

Kawamura sees a man who is also looking for someone, so he approaches him and asks if he is Mr. Yamashita.

K: _____ 1

The man says he is not.

M1: _____ 2

Kawamura apologizes.

K: _____ 3

In the meantime, a different man comes to Kawamura and asks if he is Kawamura.

M2: _____ 4

Kawamura answers yes and asks the man his name.

K: _____ 5

The man says he is Yamashita and greets Kawamura.

Y: _____ 6

Kawamura returns the greeting and says, "Nice to meet you."

K: _____ 7

Everyday Greetings

A. What would you say in the following situations? Write the letter of the most appropriate phrase in the blank next to the description of the situation.

1. _____ It's 8:00 A.M. Professor Yokoi comes into the classroom.

2. _____ You are about to go to bed, and you say good night to your family.

3. _____ You are saying goodbye to a friend whom you will see again soon.

4. _____ You run into Professor Yokoi on campus after lunch.

5. _____ Someone has asked about your health.

6. _____ You meet your friend, whom you have not seen for about a year.

7. _____ Someone remarks that it's nice weather.

8. _____ It's 7:00 P.M. You run into Professor Yokoi at a supermarket.

a. Ja, mata.
b. Ohayoo gozaimasu.
c. Konban wa.
d. Shibaraku desu ne.
e. Okagesamade, genki desu.
f. Konnichi wa.
g. Oyasuminasai.
h. Soo desu ne.

B. What might these people be saying to each other? Write a two-line dialogue for each of the following pictures.

1.

2.

3.

4.

5.

1. A: _____ 1

   B: _____ 2

2. A: _____ 1

   B: _____ 2

3. A: _____ 1

   B: _____ 2

4. A: _____ 1

   B: _____ 2

5. A: _____ 1

   B: _____ 2

Asking What Something Is

A. Suppose that someone asked you the following questions about food. How would you answer?

1. A: Teriyaki wa nihon ryoori desu ka.

   B: Hai, _____

2. A: Biiru wa o-sake desu ka.

   B: Hai, _____

3. A: Banana wa yasai desu ka.

   B: Iie, _____ . _____ desu.

4. A: Tomato wa kudamono desu ka.

   B: _____

5. A: Sukiyaki wa Mekishiko ryoori desu ka.

   B: _____

B. What would you say in the following situations in your Japanese class? Choose your answer from the options given, writing the appropriate letters in the blanks.

1. _____ You have a question.

2. _____ You don't know the answer to a question.

3. _____ You could not understand the question because your professor was speaking too fast.

4. _____ You understood what someone told you.

5. _____ You want to know how to say "Thank you" in Japanese.

6. _____ You need a little time to think about the answer.

a. Chotto matte kudasai.
b. Shitsumon ga arimasu.
c. Wakarimashita.
d. Wakarimasen.
e. Moo ichido, onegai shimasu.
f. *Thank You* wa nihongo de nan to iimasu ka.

C. Match each picture with the classroom command that it represents.

a.

b.

c.

d.

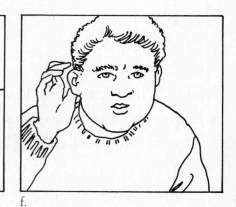

e.

f.

g.

1. _____ Hon o tojite kudasai.

2. _____ Hon o akete kudasai.

3. _____ Kiite kudasai.

4. _____ Mite kudasai.

5. _____ Itte kudasai.

6. _____ Nooto ni kaite kudasai.

7. _____ Te o agete kudasai.

D. You are a tourist in Japan. You have encountered some unfamiliar foods and beverages, which are depicted in the drawings. Complete the dialogues in which you find out what each item is called and what classification of food or drink it belongs to. Be sure that your lines make sense when taken together with what the Japanese person says.

1.   YOU: _____ 1

   JAPANESE : Udon (noodles) desu.

      YOU: _____ 2

   JAPANESE : Ee, soo desu.

2.   YOU: _____ 1

   JAPANESE: Hakutoo (white peach) desu.

      YOU: _____ 2

   JAPANESE : Ee, soo desu.

3.   YOU: _____ 1

   JAPANESE: Mugicha (barley tea) desu.

      YOU: _____ 2

   JAPANESE : Iie, chigaimasu.

HIRAGANA PRACTICE

Practice hiragana あ～お.

	hira-gana	stroke order	trace	p	r	a	c	t	i	c	e
a	あ	あ	あ								
i	い	い	い								
u	う	う	う								
e	え	え	え								
o	お	お	お								

Transcribe the following romanized words into hiragana.

1. ai (love)

   _____

2. ie (house)

   _____

3. ou (to chase)

   _____

4. au (to meet)

   _____

5. aoi (blue)

   _____

6. ue (up, top)

   _____

7. oi (nephew)

   _____

Copy these words and read them out loud.

1. いえ (house)
2. おい (nephew)
3. おう (to chase)
4. あおい (blue)
5. うえ (up, top)
6. あい (love)
7. いう (to say)

Practice hiragana か〜こ.

	hira-gana	stroke order	trace	p	r	a	c	t	i	c	e
ka	か	か	か								
ki	き	き	き								
ku	く	く	く								
ke	け	け	け								
ko	こ	こ	こ								

Transcribe the following romanized words into hiragana.

1. akai (red)

   _____

2. kiku (to listen)

   _____

3. kaku (to write)

   _____

4. koke (moss)

   _____

5. kakoi (enclosure)

   _____

6. kuki (stem)

   _____

7. koi (carp)

   _____

Copy these words and read them out loud.

1. かき (persimmon)
2. くき (stem)
3. あかい (red)
4. かこい (enclosure)
5. こい (carp)
6. こけ (moss)
7. おく (to put)
8. あき (autumn)
9. えき (train station)
10. こえ (voice)
11. かお (face)
12. いけ (pond)

Practice hiragana さ～そ.

	hiragana	stroke order	trace	p	r	a	c	t	i	c	e
sa	さ	さ	さ								
shi	し	し	し								
su	す	す	す								
se	せ	せ	せ								
so	そ	そ	そ								

Transcribe the following romanized words into hiragana.

1. shio (salt)

_____

2. sekai (world)

_____

3. kasa (umbrella)

_____

4. suika (watermelon)

_____

5. shika (deer)

_____

6. soko (bottom)

_____

7. sukoshi (little, few)

_____

Copy these words and read them out loud.

1. しあい (athletic contest)
2. かさ (umbrella)
3. さけ (rice wine)
4. すし (sushi)
5. せかい (world)
6. そこ (bottom)
7. せき (seat)
8. さか (slope)
9. あせ (sweat)
10. きそ (base)
11. うし (cow)
12. えさ (animal food)

Practice hiragana た～と.

	hira-gana	stroke order	trace	p	r	a	c	t	i	c	e
ta	た	た	た								
chi	ち	ち	ち								
tsu	つ	つ	つ								
te	て	て	て								
to	と	と	と								

Transcribe the following romanized words into hiragana.

1. takai (high)

_____

2. tsuki (moon)

_____

3. chikai (near)

_____

4. tokasu (to melt)

_____

5. tsukau (to use)

_____

6. teki (enemy)

_____

7. chikatetsu (subway)

_____

Copy these words and read them out loud.

1. ちかい (near)
2. つきあう (to associate with)
3. たかい (high)
4. てき (enemy)
5. とき (time)
6. つち (earth, ground)
7. いた (board)
8. あつい (hot)
9. こと (Japanese zither)
10. たすけて！(help!)
11. つた (ivy)
12. とし (year, age)
13. おとこ (male)
14. ちたい (zone)
15. きつい (tight)

Practice hiragana な〜の.

	hira-gana	stroke order	trace	p	r	a	c	t	i	c	e
na	な	な	な								
ni	に	に	に								
nu	ぬ	ぬ	ぬ								
ne	ね	ね	ね								
no	の	の	の								

Transcribe the following romanized words into hiragana.

1. neko (cat)

2. inu (dog)

3. kani (crab)

4. okane (money)

5. natsu (summer)

6. nanika (something)

7. nuno (cloth)

Copy these words and read them out loud.

1. なく (to cry)
2. にく (meat)
3. おかね (money)
4. ぬの (cloth)
5. ぬし (master)
6. さかな (fish)
7. のきした (under the eaves)
8. とね (name of a river)
9. なし (pear)
10. なす (eggplant)
11. にし (west)
12. しぬ (to die)
13. ぬか (rice bran)
14. たね (seed)
15. たぬき (badger)

Practice hiragana は〜ほ.

	hira-gana	stroke order	trace	p	r	a	c	t	i	c	e
ha	は	は	は								
hi	ひ	ひ	ひ								
hu	ふ	ふ	ふ								
he	へ	へ	へ								
ho	ほ	ほ	ほ								

Transcribe the following romanized words into hiragana.

1. hune (boat)

2. hashi (bridge)

3. hi (fire)

4. hoshi (star)

5. hue (flute)

6. heta (unskilled)

7. hikoku (defendant)

Copy these words and read them out loud.

1. ひと (person)
2. ほね (bone)
3. ふし (joint)
4. はこ (box)
5. ふね (boat)
6. へた (unskilled)
7. ほか (other)
8. へそ (navel)
9. へきち (remote area)
10. ふとい (thick around)
11. ほそい (thin, fine)
12. はた (loom)
13. はたけ (non-rice field)
14. そふ ([my] grandfather)
15. ひふ (skin)

Practice hiragana ま～も .

	hira-gana	stroke order	trace	p	r		a		c		t	i		c		e
ma	ま	ま	ま													
mi	み	み	み													
mu	む	む	む													
me	め	め	め													
mo	も	も	も													

Transcribe the following romanized words into hiragana.

1. musume (daughter)

_____

2. mame (bean)

_____

3. kumo (cloud)

_____

4. mimi (ear)

_____

5. mukashi (olden days)

_____

6. makoto (sincerity)

_____

7. michishio (high tide)

_____

Copy these words and read them out loud.

1. また (again)
2. みけねこ (calico cat)
3. むし (insect)
4. めし (meal)
5. かも (wild duck)
6. むすめ (daughter)
7. もも (peach)
8. みみ (ear)
9. かめ (tortoise)
10. まつ (pine)
11. はちみつ (honey)
12. もしもし (hello [on the phone])
13. あたま (head)
14. みこ (shrine maiden)
15. さめ (shark)

Practice hiragana や～よ .

	hira-gana	stroke order	trace	p	r		a		c		t	i		c		e
ya	や	や	や													
yu	ゆ	ゆ	ゆ													
yo	よ	よ	よ													

Transcribe the following romanized words into hiragana.

1. yasai (vegetable)

2. yuka (floor)

3. yotsuyu (night dew)

_____

4. yuki (snow)

5. yosoku (estimate)

6. yume (dream)

_____

7. yoyaku (reservation)

8. yakimochi (jealousy)

_____

Copy these words and read them out loud.

1. やく (bake, roast)
2. きやく (covenant)
3. ゆか (floor)
4. にえゆ (boiling water)
5. よなか (midnight)
6. かよう (to commute)
7. やきもの (pottery)
8. よそく (estimate)
9. あゆ (a kind of fish)
10. まゆ (eyebrow)
11. ふゆ (winter)
12. やたい (vendor's stall)
13. よむ (to read)
14. やま (mountain)
15. よつや (an area of Tokyo)

Practice hiragana ら〜ろ.

	hiragana	stroke order	trace	p	r	a	c	t	i	c	e
ra	ら	ら	ら								
ri	り	り	り								
ru	る	る	る								
re	れ	れ	れ								
ro	ろ	ろ	ろ								

Transcribe the following romanized words into hiragana.

1. rikai (understanding)

2. raku (comfortable)

3. roku (six)

_____

4. raretsu (enumeration)

5. rusu (not at home)

6. rokuro (lathe)

_____

7. ruiseki (accumulation)

_____

handwritten at top: + 2 %

Copy the following words and read them out loud.

handwritten: ri shi
1. り し (interest on money)   *handwritten: kariru* 2. か り る (to borrow)   3. る い す い (analogy)
handwritten: karai 4. か ら い (spicy)   5. し ろ い (white) *handwritten: shiroi*   6. ひ ろ い (wide, spacious) *handwritten: hiroii*
7. る り (lapis lazuli) *handwritten: ruri*   8. れ き し (history)   9. か る い (lightweight)
10. お さ ら い (run-through)   11. い ろ (color)   12. こ ろ す (to kill)
13. と ろ り (like a thick liquid)   14. て ら (Buddhist temple)   15. つ り (fishing)

Practice hiragana わ, を*, and ん.

	hira-gana	stroke order	trace	p	r	a	c	t	i	c	e
wa	わ	わ	わ								
o	を	を	を								
n	ん	ん	ん								

Transcribe the following romanized words into hiragana.

1. watashi (I, me)

2. wakai (young)

3. kawa (river)

4. hon (book)

5. kin (gold)

6. henka (change)

7. kinen (commemoration)

8. kin-en (no smoking)

The - (hyphen) need not be transcribed.

Copy these words and read them out loud.

1. し に ん (dead person)   2. し ん に ん (newly hired)   3. し ん い ん (true cause)
4. き ん し (forbidden)   5. お わ ん (bowl)   6. こ わ い (frightening)
7. ら い ね ん (next year)   8. に ん に く (garlic)   9. た ん い (unit)
10. ほ ん や (bookstore)   11. か わ り (substitute)   12. み か ん (Mandarin orange)
13. ふ た ん (burden)   14. わ し (handmade paper)   15. あ わ (bubble)

---

* This を is used to indicate the direct object of a verb.

Practice hiragana が～ご.

	hira-gana	p	r	a	c	t	i	c	e		
ga	が										
gi	ぎ										
gu	ぐ										
ge	げ										
go	ご										

Transcribe the following romanized words into hiragana.

1. gin (silver)

_____

2. gengo (language)

_____

3. guai (condition)

_____

4. gogo (P.M.)

_____

5. giron (argument)

_____

6. sagasu (to look for)

_____

7. hiragana

_____

Copy these words and read them out loud.

1. がまん (putting up with)
2. はぎしり (grinding one's teeth)
3. にほんご (Japanese language)
4. かげ (shadow)
5. ぐんたい (the military)
6. ごみ (trash)
7. らいげつ (next month)
8. おんがく (music)
9. かぐ (furniture)
10. が (moth)
11. あご (chin)
12. えんげき (acting)
13. そそぐ (to pour)
14. すぎ (cedar)
15. げた (Japanese clogs)

Practice hiragana さ〜ぞ.

	hira-gana	p	r	a	c	t	i	c	e	
za	さ									
ji	じ									
zu	ず									
ze	ぜ									
zo	ぞ									

Transcribe the following romanized words into hiragana.

1. kazu (number)

_____

2. zaru (basket)

_____

3. zatsuji (routine duties)

_____

4. jikan (hour)

_____

5. jiken (incident)

_____

6. zokugo (slang)

_____

7. zentai (whole)

_____

Copy these words and read them out loud.

1. ずるい (sneaky)
2. じんけん (human rights)
3. ひざ (knee)
4. じこく (time, hour)
5. かぜ (wind)
6. かぞく (family)
7. ぎんざ (an area of Tokyo)
8. おじ (uncle)
9. かずかず (numerous)
10. ぜんぜん (not at all)
11. ざんねん (regrettable)
12. なぞ (riddle)

Practice hiragana だ～ど.

(ぢ and づ are limited in use compared with じ and ず.)

	hira-gana	p	r	a	c	t	i	c	e
da	だ								
ji	ぢ								
zu	づ								
de	で								
do	ど								

Transcribe the following romanized words into hiragana.

1. dame (no good)

_____

2. hanaji (nosebleed)

_____

3. doku (poison)

_____

4. kizuku (to notice)

_____

5. dekiru (be able to)

_____

6. denwa (telephone)

_____

7. daidokoro (kitchen)

_____

Copy these words and read them out loud.

1. かだん (flower bed)
2. たどん (briquet)
3. わかづま (young wife)
4. みぢか (close at hand)
5. しんてん (sanctuary)
6. だます (deceive)
7. どれ (which one)
8. めだつ (to be noticeable)
9. だけ (only)
10. どこ (where)
11. できごと (event)
12. つづく (continue)

Practice hiragana ば～ぼ.

	hira-gana	practice									
ba	ば										
bi	び										
bu	ぶ										
be	べ										
bo	ぼ										

Transcribe the following romanized words into hiragana.

1. kaban (bag)

2. benri (convenient)

3. kabi (mold)

4. bonchi (basin)

5. bitoku (virtue)

6. haba (width)

7. bunka (culture)

Copy these words and read them out loud.

1. かば (hippopotamus)
2. びじん (beautiful woman)
3. ぶし (warrior)
4. べんかい (vindication)
5. ぼくとつ (simplicity)
6. ぶんべん (childbirth)
7. びぶん (differential)
8. かびん (vase)
9. おぼん (the Bon festival)
10. ばか (fool)
11. くべつ (distinction)
12. ぼこくご (native language)

Practice hiragana ぱ～ぽ.

	hira-gana	p	r	a	c	t	i	c	e
pa	ぱ								
pi	ぴ								
pu	ぷ								
pe	ぺ								
po	ぽ								

Transcibe the following romanized words into hiragana.

1. yutanpo (hot-water bottle)

   _____

2. pakutsuku (to bite at)

   _____

3. petenshi (impostor)

   _____

4. pinhane (kickback)

   _____

5. kanpai (cheers)

   _____

6. sanpo (taking a walk)

   _____

7. kinpen (neighborhood)

   _____

Copy these words and read them out loud.

1. かんぱん (deck)
2. えんぴつ (pencil)
3. さんぷん (three minutes)
4. きんぺん (neighborhood)
5. さんぽ (taking a walk)
6. ざんぱん (leftovers)
7. ぽつぽつ (in drops)
8. あんぴ (well-being)
9. おんぱ (sound wave)
10. なんぱ (shipwreck)
11. こんぽん (source)
12. しんぷ (Catholic priest)

Practice the following hiragana.

	hi ra ga na	p	r	a	c	t	i	c	e
kya	きゃ								
kyu	きゅ								
kyo	きょ								
sha	しゃ								
shu	しゅ								
sho	しょ								
cha	ちゃ								
chu	ちゅ								
cho	ちょ								
nya	にゃ								
nyu	にゅ								
nyo	にょ								
hya	ひゃ								
hyu	ひゅ								
hyo	ひょ								

* Write small characters in the lower left corner when writing horizontally.

	hi ra ga na	p	r	a	c	t	i	c	e
mya	み や								
myu	み ゆ								
myo	み よ								
rya	り や								
ryu	り ゆ								
ryo	り よ								
gya	ぎ や								
gyu	ぎ ゆ								
gyo	ぎ よ								
ja	じ や								
ju	じ ゆ								
jo	じ よ								
bya	び や								
byu	び ゆ								
byo	び よ								

	hi ra ga na	p	r	a	c	t	i	c	e
pya	ぴゃ								
pyu	ぴゅ								
pyo	ぴょ								

Transcribe the following romanized words into hiragana.

1. kyaku (guest)

2. shuhu (housewife)

3. jisho (dictionary)

4. chokusetsu (direct)

5. hyaku (hundred)

6. shain (company employee)

7. kyoka (permission)

8. myaku (pulse)

9. ryokan (inn)

10. ryakusu (to abbreviate)

11. gyomin (fisherman)

12. gyaku (reverse)

13. kanja (patient)

14. joshi (particle)

Copy these words and read them out loud.

1. きゃくしゃ (passenger train)
2. じしょ (dictionary)
3. しゃくや (rented house)
4. しょり (management)
5. しゅみ (hobby)
6. きんぎょ (goldfish)
7. ひゃくにん (one hundred people)
8. しょみん (populace)
9. ひしょ (secretary)
10. りょかん (inn)
11. じゅり (acceptance)
12. じゅけん (taking a test)
13. こんにゃく (a kind of vegetable)
14. さんびゃく (three hundred)
15. りゃくだつ (plunder)

Transcribe the following romanized words that contain double vowels into hiragana.

1. kooshoo (negotiation)

2. kyuuryoo (salary)

3. bangoo (number)

4. eego (English)

5. Chuugoku (China)

6. bunpoo (grammar)

7. getsuyoobi (Monday)

8. tooi (far) *

9. kuuki (air)

10. heewa (peace)

11. ookii (big) *

12. huutoo (envelope)

13. kakee (family finance)

14. kyuuka (vacation)

15. okaasan (mother)

16. ojiisan (grandfather)

17. reezooko (refrigerator)

18. sensee (teacher)

19. utsukushii (beautiful)

20. gyuunyuu (cow's milk)

21. shuujin (prisoner)

22. meeshi (name card)

23. Tookyoo (Tokyo)

24. Oosaka (Osaka) *

25. suugaku (mathematics)

26. jinkoo (population)

27. hontoo (really)

28. doroboo (thief)

29. chiisai (small)

30. huuhu (married couple)

Transcribe the following romanized words that contain double consonants into hiragana.

1. hakkiri (clearly)

2. tassha (healthy)

3. sotto (softly)

4. happyaku (eight hundred)

---

* These words are spelled with an actual "oo" instead of with "ou."

5. kokki (national flag)

_____

6. shippai (failure)

_____

7. kitto (surely)

_____

8. kitte (stamp)

_____

9. kesshi (desperate)

_____

10. hossa (heart attack)

_____

11. sekkachi (hasty person)

_____

12. shakkin (debt)

_____

NOTE: The double *n* is not represented by the small つ. In this case, the first *n* is represented by ん.

shinnen (new year) → しんねん   hannin (criminal) → はんにん
konnyaku (devil's tongue, a kind of vegetable) → こんにゃく.   kanna (carpenter's plane) → かんな

Copy these words and read them out loud.

1. きって (stamp)
2. けっし (desperate)
3. いっち (concurrence)
4. すっかり (entirely)
5. はっぷん (eight minutes)
6. しゃっくり (hiccough)
7. ひょっとこ (jester)
8. ひっぱる (to pull)
9. かっこ (parentheses)
10. じっこう (implementation)
11. はっぱ (leaf)
12. けってい (decision)
13. さっか (writer)
14. やっと (at last)
15. とっきょ (patent)

HIRAGANA DERIVATIONS

The hiragana are derived from simplified, cursive forms of the kanji.

		k	s	t	n	h	m	y	r	w	n
a	あ 安	か 加	さ 左	た 太	な 奈	は 波	ま 末	や 也	ら 良	わ 和	ん 尤
i	い 以	き 幾	し 之	ち 知	に 仁	ひ 比	み 美		り 利		
u	う 宇	く 久	す 寸	つ 川	ぬ 奴	ふ 不	む 武	ゆ 由	る 留		
e	え 衣	け 計	せ 世	て 天	ね 祢	へ 部	め 女		れ 礼		
o	お 於	こ 己	そ 曽	と 止	の 乃	ほ 保	も 毛	よ 与	ろ 呂	を 遠	

PART TWO

Listening Comprehension Activities

Asking and Giving Telephone Numbers

A. You will hear a series of statements about the phone number of each of the following people. Write down the number next to the person's name.

1. Antonio Coronado: _____

2. Peggy Yu: _____

3. Jin Mi Kim: _____

4. Hans Kraus: _____

5. Ryan Scott: _____

B. You will hear three dialogues in which a Japanese student newly arrived at an American university asks another Japanese student for the phone numbers of various campus locations. Write the name of each building or office next to its phone number.

1. 856-1293: _____

2. 725-0601: _____

3. 722-8740: _____

Asking and Telling Time

A. Listen to the tape and identify the times given in the following four statements, matching Column I with Column II.

I

1. _____ 9:00 A.M.

2. _____ 6:30 P.M.

3. _____ 7:30

4. _____ 8:00

II

a. now
b. party
c. Japanese class
d. supper

B. Listen to Professor Arai talk about her schedule for today, and fill in the blanks with the appropriate times.

USEFUL VOCABULARY

kyoo	today
···kara	from . . .
···made	until . . .
yasumi	a break

Professor Arai teaches Japanese at _____, _____, and

_____. She has a break between _____ and _____ and

has lunch between _____ and _____. At _____, she

has a meeting. She will go shopping _____.

Talking About Likes and Preferences

A. Listen to the descriptions of Midori Momoi's and Ryan Scott's likes and dislikes. Then mark each statement below with an *M* if it is true of Momoi and *S* if it is true of Scott.

USEFUL VOCABULARY

demo	*but*
mo	*also, too*
daisuki(na)	*to like very much, to love*
daikirai(na)	*to dislike, to hate*
soshite	*and then*

1. _____ loves Japanese food.

2. _____ doesn't like fish.

3. _____ likes beer.

4. _____ hates studying.

5. _____ likes movies.

6. _____ likes swimming.

7. _____ likes coffee and Coke.

8. _____ likes parties.

9. _____ doesn't like sake.

10. _____ likes fruit.

B. Listen as Masaru Honda, a reporter, interviews Himiko, a popular but flamboyantly eccentric singer and actress. After hearing the conversation, cross out the things Himiko doesn't like and circle the things she likes.

music   studying   tennis   Italian food   cooking   Japanese food   swimming

Writing Activities

Numbers Up to 20

Complete each equation.

1. $2 + 5 = 7$ ni tasu _____ wa nana

2. $4 + 9 = 13$ yon tasu _____ wa juu-san

3. $3 + 1 = 4$ san _____ ichi wa yon

4. $8 - 6 = 2$ _____ hiku roku wa ni

5. $30 - 10 = 20$ sanjuu _____ juu wa nijuu

6. $5 \times 6 = 30$ _____ kakeru roku wa sanjuu

7. $2 \times 7 = 14$ ni kakeru nana wa _____

8. $20 \div 4 = 5$ nijuu waru yon wa _____

9. $24 \div 8 = 3$ nijuu-shi waru _____ wa san

10. $18 \div 9 = 2$ juu-hachi _____ kyuu wa ni

Asking and Giving Telephone Numbers

Complete the dialogue, using the following information about Machida's and Brown's telephone numbers.

Machida   492-6592
Buraun   672-0185

BROWN: Machida-san no denwa bangoo wa?

MACHIDA: _____1 kyuu ni no roku _____2 kyuu ni desu.

BROWN: Yon kyuu ni no roku go kyuu ni desu ka?

MACHIDA: Hai, soo desu. Buraun-san no _____3 wa?

BROWN: Roku _____4 ni _____5 zero ichi hachi go desu.

MACHIDA: Roku ichi ni no zero ichi hachi go desu ka.

BROWN: Iie, _____6.

MACHIDA: Moo ichido onegai shimasu.

BROWN: Roku nana ni no _____7 ichi _____7 go desu.

MACHIDA: Wakarimashita.

Asking and Telling Time

A. Ima nan-ji desu ka? Which is the clock that this person is looking at? Match each clock with the statements about the time of day.

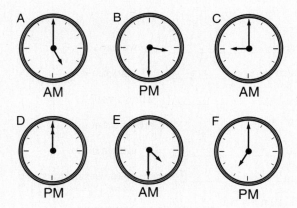

1. _____ Ima gozen go-ji desu. Asa desu.

2. _____ Ima gozen ku-ji desu. Asa desu.

3. _____ Ima gogo shichi-ji desu. Yoru desu.

4. _____ Ima gogo san-ji han desu. Hiru desu.

5. _____ Ima gogo juu ni-ji desu. Yoru desu.

6. _____ Ima gozen yo-ji han desu. Asa desu.

B. Complete the following dialogues, using the information in the table below.

	AM											PM											
Tokyo	1	2	3	4	5	6	7	8	9	10	11	12	1	2	3	4	5	6	7	8	9	10	11	12

	AM				PM								AM							
Los Angeles	8	9	10	11	12	1	2	3	4	5	6	7	8	9	10	11	12	1	2	3	4	5	6	7

	PM					AM													PM			
Paris	5	6	7	8	9	10	11	12	1	2	3	4	5	6	7	8	9	10	11	12	1	2	3	4

1. (A conversation in Japan)

    A: Ima nan-ji desu ka.

    B: Gogo roku-ji desu.

    A: Huransu wa _____1 nan-ji desu ka.

    B: Eeto, _____2 desu.

    A: Gozen _____3 desu ka.

    B: Hai, soo desu. Huransu wa ima _____4 desu.

2. (A conversation in Los Angeles)

   A: Ima _____1 desu ka.

   B: Gogo yo-ji desu.

   A: Tookyoo wa _____2 nan-ji desu ka.

   B: Eeto, _____3 desu.

   A: Gozen _____4 desu ka.

   B: Hai, soo desu. Tookyoo wa ima _____5 desu.

C. Complete the dialogues, using the information on the following schedule.

6:30	Exercise
7:30	Breakfast
9:00	Japanese class
1:00	Lunch
4:00	Meeting
5:30	Taking a walk
7:00	Dinner
7:30	Date

1. A: Nihongo no kurasu wa nan-ji kara desu ka.

   B: _____ kara desu.

2. B: Asagohan wa nan-ji desu ka.

   B: _____ desu.

3. A: Undoo wa nan-ji kara desu ka.

   B: _____ kara desu.

4. A: Deeto wa nan-ji kara desu ka.

   B: _____ kara desu.

5. A: Yuugohan wa nan-ji desu ka.

   B: _____ desu.

6. A: Sanpo wa nan-ji kara desu ka.

   B: _____ kara desu.

7. A: Miitingu wa nan-ji kara desu ka.

   B: _____kara desu.

8. A: Hirugohan wa nan-ji desu ka.

   B: _____ desu.

D. Please answer the following questions. (Be sure to add A.M. and P.M. when stating the times.)

1. Anata no denwa bangoo wa. _____

2. Ima nan-ji desu ka. _____

3. Shikago wa ima nan-ji desu ka. _____

4. San Huranshisuko wa. _____

5. Jaa, Nyuu Yooku wa. _____

E. Write up your own schedule for tomorrow, listing five to eight activities, and trade schedules with a classmate. Write five questions about your classmate's schedule in his or her workbook in the blanks below labeled "classmate". Then take your own workbook back and answer your classmate's questions in the blanks labeled "you."

EXAMPLE: breakfast   7:00 A.M.

      CLASSMATE: Asagohan wa nan-ji desu ka.
          YOU: Shichi-ji desu.

1. CLASSMATE: _____ 1

        YOU: _____ 2

2. CLASSMATE: _____ 1

        YOU: _____ 2

3. CLASSMATE: _____ 1

        YOU: _____ 2

4. CLASSMATE: _____ 1

        YOU: _____ 2

5. CLASSMATE: _____ 1

        YOU: _____ 2

Talking About Likes and Dislikes

A. Complete the following conversations by answering the questions, expressing your own particular likes and dislikes.

EXAMPLE: A: Aisu kuriimu ga suki desu ka.
          B: Ee, toku ni chokoreeto aisu kuriimu ga suki desu.

1. A: Eega ga suki desu ka.

    B: Ee, toku ni _____ ga suki desu.

2. A: Undoo ga suki desu ka.

    B: Ee, toku ni _____ ga suki desu.

3. A: Yasai ga suki desu ka.

    B: Iie, kirai desu. Toku ni _____ ga kirai desu.

4. A: Benkyoo ga suki desu ka.

 B: Iie, kirai desu. Toku ni _____ ga kirai desu.

5. A: Nihon ryoori ga _____ desu ka.

 B: Ee, toku ni _____ ga suki desu.

6. A: Supootsu ga suki desu ka.

 B: Ee, toku ni _____ ga suki desu.

B. Trade workbooks with a classmate. Write questions in which you ask your classmate whether he or she likes a certain thing in each category given. Then take back your own workbook and answer the questions your classmate has written.

EXAMPLE: (music) Q: Kurashikku ga suki desu ka.
     A: Iie, kirai desu.

1. (sports)

 Q: _____ 1

 A: _____ 2

2. (Japanese food)

 Q: _____ 1

 A: _____ 2

3. (drink)

 Q: _____ 1

 A: _____ 2

4. (television program)

 Q: _____ 1

 A: _____ 2

KATAKANA PRACTICE

Practice katakana ア〜ノ.

	kata-kana	stroke order	trace	p	r	a	c	t	i	c	e
a	ア	ア	ア								
i	イ	イ	イ								
u	ウ	ウ	ウ								
e	エ	エ	エ								
o	オ	オ	オ								
ka	カ	カ	カ								
ki	キ	キ	キ								
ku	ク	ク	ク								
ke	ケ	ケ	ケ								
ko	コ	コ	コ								
sa	サ	サ	サ								
shi	シ	シ	シ								
su	ス	ス	ス								
se	セ	セ	セ								
so	ソ	ソ	ソ								

	kata-kana	stroke order	trace	p	r	a	c	t	i	c	e
ta	タ	タ	タ								
chi	チ	チ	チ								
tsu	ツ	ツ	ツ								
te	テ	テ	テ								
to	ト	ト	ト								
na	ナ	ナ	ナ								
ni	ニ	ニ	ニ								
nu	ヌ	ヌ	ヌ								
ne	ネ	ネ	ネ								
no	ノ	ノ	ノ								

Transcribe the following romanized words into katakana. Not all of them are in common use in Japan; some are found only in compound words or phrases.

1. aisu (ice)

    _____

3. kakao (cacao)

    _____

5. kisu (kiss)

    _____

7. kokoa (cocoa)

    _____

2. ekisaito (excite)

    _____

4. kiui (kiwi)

    _____

6. kenia (Kenya)

    _____

8. sauna (sauna)

    _____

9. shinia (senior)

_____

10. sukai (sky)

_____

11. sonata (sonata)

_____

12. tsuisuto (twist)

_____

13. naito (night)

_____

14. tekisuto (textbook)

_____

15. tai (Thailand)

_____

16. suisu (Switzerland)

_____

17. oashisu (oasis)

_____

18. saiki (psyche)

_____

19. sukuea (square)

_____

20. naisu (nice)

_____

21. taitsu (tights)

_____

22. tsuna (tuna)

_____

23. katsu (cutlet)

_____

24. sutoa (store)

_____

Practice katakana ハ〜ン.

	kata-kana	stroke order	trace	p	r	a	c	t	i	c	e
ha	ハ	ハ	ハ								
hi	ヒ	ヒ	ヒ								
hu	フ	フ	フ								
he	ヘ	ヘ	ヘ								
ho	ホ	ホ	ホ								
ma	マ	マ	マ								
mi	ミ	ミ	ミ								
mu	ム	ム	ム								
me	メ	メ	メ								
mo	モ	モ	モ								
ya	ヤ	ヤ	ヤ								
yu	ユ	ユ	ユ								
yo	ヨ	ヨ	ヨ								

	kata-kana	stroke order	trace	p	r	a	c	t	i	c	e
ra	ラ	ラ	ラ								
ri	リ	リ	リ								
ru	ル	ル	ル								
re	レ	レ	レ								
ro	ロ	ロ	ロ								
wa	ワ	ウ	ワ								
o	ヲ	ヲ	ラ								
n	ン	ン	ン								

Transcribe the following romanized words into katakana.

1. haichi (Haiti)

_____

2. huransu (France)

_____

3. remon (lemon)

_____

4. warutsu (waltz)

_____

5. waihu (wife)

_____

6. kurisumasu (Christmas)

_____

7. washinton (Washington)

_____

8. airon (iron)

_____

9. hawai (Hawaii)

_____

10. mekishiko (Mexico)

_____

11. sanhuranshisuko (San Francisco)

_____

12. irinoi (Illinois)

_____

13. mosukuwa (Moscow)

_____

14. shiatoru (Seattle)

_____

Name _____ Date _____ Class _____

Practice katakana ガ～ボ.

	kata-kana	p	r	a	c	t	i	c	e	
ga	ガ									
gi	ギ									
gu	グ									
ge	ゲ									
go	ゴ									
za	ザ									
ji	ジ									
zu	ズ									
ze	ゼ									
zo	ゾ									
da	ダ									
ji	ヂ									
zu	ヅ									
de	デ									
do	ド									

	kata-kana											
		p	r	a	c	t	i	c	e			
ba	バ											
bi	ビ											
bu	ブ											
be	ベ											
bo	ボ											
pa	パ											
pi	ピ											
pu	プ											
pe	ペ											
po	ポ											

Transcribe the following romanized words into katakana.

1. gesuto (guest)

_____

2. baiorin (violin)

_____

3. posuto (mail box)

_____

4. daibingu (diving)

_____

5. doraibu (drive)

_____

6. pepushi (Pepsi)

_____

7. supein (Spain)

_____

8. parasoru (parasol)

_____

9. bikini (bikini)

_____

10. gumu (Guam)

_____

11. pinpon (Ping-Pong)

_____

12. bikutoria (Victoria)

_____

Practice the following katakana.

	ka ta ka na		p	r	a	c	t	i	c	e
kya	キ	ャ								
kyu	キ	ュ								
kyo	キ	ョ								
sha	シ	ャ								
shu	シ	ュ								
sho	シ	ョ								
cha	チ	ャ								
chu	チ	ュ								
cho	チ	ョ								
nya	ニ	ャ								
nyu	ニ	ュ								
nyo	ニ	ョ								
hya	ヒ	ャ								
hyu	ヒ	ュ								
hyo	ヒ	ョ								

✳ Write small characters in the lower left corner when writing horizontally.

	ka ta ka na		p r a c t i c e							
mya	ミ	ャ								
myu	ミ	ユ								
myo	ミ	ョ								
rya	リ	ャ								
ryu	リ	ユ								
ryo	リ	ョ								
gya	ギ	ャ								
gyu	ギ	ユ								
gyo	ギ	ョ								
ja	ジ	ャ								
ju	ジ	ユ								
jo	ジ	ョ								
bya	ビ	ャ								
byu	ビ	ユ								
byo	ビ	ョ								

	ka ta ka na	p	r	a	c	t	i	c	e
pya	ピャ								
pyu	ピュ								
pyo	ピョ								

Transcribe the following romanized words into katakana.

1. kyabetsu (cabbage)

_____

2. jakaruta (Jakarta)

_____

3. gyanburu (gamble)

_____

4. jointo (joint)

_____

5. jogingu (jogging)

_____

6. rosanjerusu (Los Angeles)

_____

7. jazu (jazz)

_____

8. kyajuaru (casual)

_____

Transcribe the following romanized words that contain double vowels into katakana. Remember that double vowels are indicated by writing a "ー" after the vowel to be lengthened.

1. koohii (coffee)

_____

2. hurawaa (flower)

_____

3. meetoru (meter)

_____

4. biiru (beer)

_____

5. juusaa (juicer)

_____

6. chaamingu (charming)

_____

7. tawaa (tower)

_____

8. shiitsu (sheet)

_____

9. roodoshoo (road show)

_____

10. nyuusu (news)

_____

11. chiizu (cheese)

_____

12. oobaakooto (overcoat)

_____

Transcribe the following romanized words that contain double consonants into katakana. Remember that double consonants are indicated by writing a small " ッ " before the consonant to be doubled.

1. kukkii (cookie)

_____

2. kyatto huudo (cat food)

_____

3. piinattsu (peanut)

_____

4. torakku (track)

_____

5. jaketto (jacket)

_____

6. kicchin (kitchen)

_____

7. beddo (bed)

_____

8. burudoggu (bulldog)

_____

9. burijji (bridge)

_____

10. happii (happy)

_____

What do the following katakana words mean?

1. チョコレート

_____

2. オーストラリア

_____

3. ドリーム

_____

4. ミュージック

_____

5. カセットテープ

_____

6. レストラン

_____

7. シャワー

_____

8. チーズバーガー

_____

9. セーター

_____

10. バレーボール

_____

11. ショッピング

_____

12. アメリカ

_____

13. デパート

_____

14. カー・ステレオ

_____

15. シャツ

_____

16. ビジネス

_____

17. クレジット・カード

_____

18. テスト

_____

Practice the following katakana.

	ka ta ka na		p	r	a	c	t	i	c	e
wi	ウ	ィ								
we	ウ	ェ								
wo	ウ	ォ								
she	シ	ェ								
che	チ	ェ								
tsa	ツ	ァ								
tsi	ツ	ィ								
tse	ツ	ェ								
tso	ツ	ォ								
ti	テ	ィ								
tu	ト	ゥ								
hye	ヒ	ェ								
fa	フ	ァ								
fi	フ	ィ								
fe	フ	ェ								

* Write small characters in the lower left corner when writing horizontally.

Practice the following katakana.

	ka ta ka na		p	r	a	c	t	i	c	e
fo	フ	オ								
je	ジ	エ								
di	デ	ィ								
dyu	デ	ュ								
du	ド	ゥ								
kwa	ク	ァ								
kwo	ク	ォ								
va	ヴ	ァ								
vi	ヴ	ィ								
ve	ヴ	エ								
vo	ヴ	オ								

_____
* Write small characters in the lower left corner when writing horizontally.

Transcribe the following romanized words into katakana.

1. faam (farm)

   _____

2. chero (cello)

   _____

3. aamuchea (arm chair)

   _____

4. paatii (party)

   _____

5. faibu (five)

   _____

6. dyuo (duo)

   _____

7. sheebaa (shaver)

_____

8. weeto (weight)

_____

9. fiijii (Fiji)

_____

10. fensu (fence)

_____

11. woo (war)

_____

12. janbo (jumbo)

_____

13. chekku (check)

_____

14. jesuchaa (gesture)

_____

15. sheekaa (shaker)

_____

16. fooku (fork)

_____

17. dyuetto (duet)

_____

18. birudingu (building)

_____

19. wokka (vodka)

_____

20. viinasu (Venus)

_____

KATAKANA DERIVATIONS

The katakana were created from parts of the kanji.

		k	s	t	n	h	m	y	r	w	n
a	ア 阿	カ 加	サ 散	タ 多	ナ 奈	ハ 八	マ 末	ヤ 也	ラ 良	ワ 和	ン 尓
i	イ 伊	キ 幾	シ 之	チ 千	ニ 仁	ヒ 比	ミ 三		リ 利		
u	ウ 宇	ク 久	ス 須	ツ 川	ヌ 奴	フ 不	ム 牟	ユ 由	ル 流		
e	エ 江	ケ 介	セ 世	テ 天	ネ 祢	ヘ 部	メ 女		レ 礼		
o	オ 於	コ 己	ソ 曽	ト 止	ノ 乃	ホ 保	モ 毛	ヨ 與	ロ 呂	ヲ 乎	

PART THREE

Listening Comprehension Activities

Asking Locations

A. Listen as customers ask for directions at the information counter in a department store, and find out where the following places are located. Then indicate each location by writing its number in the appropriate place on the drawing.

USEFUL VOCABULARY

otearai   *restroom*

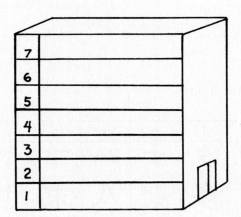

1. book department   2. shoe department   3. restrooms

B. Listen to the dialogue between Midori Momoi and Hans Kraus. Then read the statements and mark each one either true (T) or false (F).

USEFUL VOCABULARY

kono   *this*
tatemono   *building*
hontoo ni   *really, truly*

1. _____ Professor Arai's office is in this building.

2. _____ Hans thinks that this building is a little inconvenient because it is far from the cafeteria.

3. _____ The library is near this building.

4. _____ Hans thinks that this building is inconvenient because it has only a snack bar.

5. _____ There are telephones in this building.

Asking About Existence and Price

A. Listen as Brown and Machida order lunch at a restaurant near their university in Tokyo. Then read the statements below and mark them either true (T) or false (F).

USEFUL VOCABULARY

zenbu de   *in total*

1. _____ Brown will have curry and rice for lunch.

2. _____ *Gyuudon* consists of beef and rice.

3. _____ Salad costs 350 yen.

4. _____ Brown will pay 620 yen in total.

5. _____ Machida will pay 450 yen.

B. The following scene takes place at a busy kiosk in Tokyo Station. Listen to the conversations between the attendant and a series of five customers, and then write down the price of each item in the blanks provided.

USEFUL VOCABULARY

zasshi   *magazine*
donna . . .   *what kind of . . .*

1. cola   _____ yen

2. orange juice   _____ yen

3. cigarettes   _____ yen

4. magazine   _____ yen

Talking About Daily Activities

A. Listen to Peggy Yu talk about her daily activities and indicate at what time she does the following.

EXAMPLE: 6:00   get up

1. _____ go to school

2. _____ have lunch

3. _____ go to Japanese class

4. _____ go home

5. _____ study in the library

6. _____ eat breakfast

7. _____ watch TV

8. _____ go to bed

9. _____ eat supper

B. Listen as Ryan Scott talks about his daily activities. Then read the following statements and mark them either true (T) or false (F).

USEFUL VOCABULARY

ya	*and (so forth)*
osoku	*(adv.) late*
ga	*but, although*
. . . to	*with . . .*
koro / goro	*about, around*

Scott:

1. _____ exercises every morning after breakfast.

2. _____ thinks the Japanese class is a little too early for him.

3. _____ is sometimes late for the class because he doesn't like the professor.

4. _____ eats lunch around noon.

5. _____ often studies at the library with his friends.

6. _____ plays sports in the afternoon.

7. _____ eats dinner at home.

8. _____ doesn't go out at night.

9. _____ doesn't study at home.

10. _____ is a serious student.

C. Listen as Honda continues interviewing Himiko. Then complete each sentence by circling the correct word or phrase.

USEFUL VOCABULARY

. . . kara	*because, since*
shinbun	*newspaper*
renshuu	*practice*
sore kara	*then, afterwards*

Himiko:

1. gets up (early / late) every day.
2. eats (breakfast / lunch).
3. eats a (light / heavy) meal.
4. (works / relaxes) in the afternoon.
5. (does / does not) exercise.
6. (reads / sleeps) before work.
7. works (in the morning / at night).

Writing Activities

Asking Location

A. Complete the following dialogues, referring to the store directory below, which tells what floor each item is found on.

8	hon
7	teeburu
6	seetaa
5	tokee/mannenhitsu
4	doresu
3	kasa
2	shatsu/sokkusu
1	kutsu/tebukuro
B1	aisu kuriimu

1. A: Sumimasen. Hon wa doko desu ka.

   B: Hai, hon wa _____1 desu.

   A: A, soo desu ka. Arigatoo gozaimasu.

   B: _____2.

2. A: Sumimasen. Shatsu wa _____1 desu ka.

   B: Hai, shatsu wa _____2 desu.

   A: A, soo desu ka. _____3.

   B: Doo itashimashite.

3. A: _____1. Teeburu wa doko desu ka.

   B: Hai, _____2 wa _____3 desu.

   A: A, _____4. Arigatoo gozaimasu.

   B: Doo itashimashite.

4. A: Sumimasen. _____1 wa doko desu ka.

   B: Hai, _____2 wa ik-kai desu.

   A: A, soo desu ka. _____3.

   B: Doo itashimashite.

5. A: Sumimasen. Seetaa wa _____1 desu ka.

   B: Hai, seetaa wa _____2 desu.

   A: A, soo desu ka. Arigatoo gozaimasu.

   B: _____3.

B. Here is a diagram of Yasuda International Company's offices. Answer the questions based on the diagram.

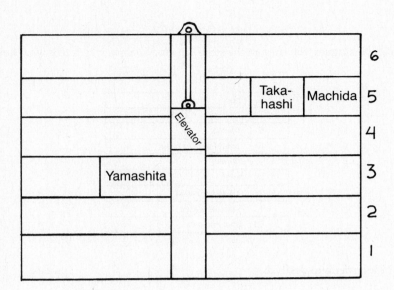

1. Machida-san no ofisu wa doko desu ka.

   _____

2. Takahashi-san no ofisu ni chikai desu ka.

   _____

3. Yamashita-san no ofisu ni chikai desu ka.

   _____

4. Jaa, Yamashita-san no ofisu wa doko desu ka.

   _____

5. Yamashita-san no ofisu wa erebeetaa kara tooi desu ka.

   _____

Numbers Up to 9,999

Match each arithmetical expression with its correct answer.

8300 + 382 = (1) _____

400 ÷ 50 = (2) _____

65 + 200 = (3) _____

40 × 70 = (4) _____

5000 − 3500 = (5) _____

9999 ÷ 3 = (6) _____

7700 − 10 = (7) _____

8 × 100 = (8) _____

(a) nihyaku rokujuu go
(b) sanzen sanbyaku sanjuu san
(c) sen gohyaku
(d) hachi
(e) hassen roppyaku hachijuu ni
(f) nanasen roppyaku kyuujuu
(g) happyaku
(h) nisen happyaku

Asking About Existence / Asking About Price

A. Complete the following dialogues, basing your answers on the menu below.

Menu

supagetti	750 en	koohii	380 en
piza	500 en	juusu	400 en
suupu	450 en	koora	400 en
suteeki	890 en		
teriyaki	790 en		
sarada	370 en		

1. A: Sumimasen. Supagetti wa arimasu ka.

    B: Hai, arimasu.

    A: Ja, supagetti o _____ 1.

    B: Hai, _____ 2 en desu.

2. A: Sumimasen. Piza wa _____ 1 ka.

    B: Hai, _____ 2.

    A: Ja, piza o onegai shimasu.

    B: Hai, _____ 3 en desu.

3. A: _____ 1. Tenpura wa arimasu ka.

    B: Sumimasen ga, chotto···

A: Ja, teriyaki wa _____ 2 ka.

B: Hai, _____ 3.

A: Ja, teriyaki _____ 4 onegai shimasu.

B: Hai, _____ 5 en desu.

4. A: _____ 1. Aisu kuriimu _____ 2 arimasu ka.

B: Sumimasen ga, _____ 3···

A: Ja, koohii _____ 4 arimasu ka.

B: Hai, arimasu.

A: Ja, koohii _____ 5 onegai shimasu.

B: Hai, 380 _____ 6 desu.

5. A: Sumimasen. Hanbaagaa wa arimasu ka.

B: _____ 1.

A: _____ 2, suteeki wa arimasu ka.

B: Hai, arimasu.

A: _____ 3, suteeki o _____ 4.

B: Hai, _____ 5 desu.

B. Choose the most appropriate response from the second column.

1. ____ Fisshu baagaa wa arimasu ka.

2. ____ Ikura desu ka.

3. ____ Chiizu baagaa o onegai shimasu.

4. ____ Onion ringu wa ikaga desu ka.

    a. 350 en desu.
    b. Hai, arimasu.
    c. Kekkoo desu.
    d. Arigatoo gozaimasu. 330 en desu.

C. In the first column are some statements and courtesy phrases, each of which could be the response to a question or courtesy phrase in the second column.

1. ____ 560 en desu.

2. ____ Sumimasen ga, chotto . . .

3. ____ Arigatoo gozaimasu.

4. ____ Kekkoo desu.

5. ____ Hai, hon wa yon-kai desu.

6. ____ Mejiro desu.

7. ____ Iie, chotto tooi desu.

    a. Hon wa doko desu ka.
    b. Koora to keeki o onegai shimasu.
    c. Tokee wa arimasu ka.
    d. Kono seetaa wa ikura desu ka.
    e. Daigaku ni chikai desu ka.
    f. Chin-san no uchi wa doko desu ka.
    g. Hurenchi hurai wa ikaga desu.

D. Large department stores in Japan usually have a restaurant floor, sometimes containing several different restaurants. Window displays featuring realistic plastic models of the food allow shoppers to see what each restaurant offers. After choosing what they want to eat, customers buy tickets for the food from the cashier, sit down at a table, and wait for the waiter or waitress to take their tickets and bring the meal.

Using this list as a menu, make up a conversation between yourself and the cashier. You may want to review Dialogues 3 – 5 in your main text before doing this exercise.

Situation: You're at a department store, and you want to have something to eat and something to drink. You go to the cashier and order food and a beverage. You find that the food item you want is sold out, so you choose something else. Then you order a drink and pay the correct amount.

Menyuu

karee raisu	580
sandoicchi	600
supagetti	550
oyako donburi	600
yakiniku teeshoku	900
okosama ranchi	450
sushi moriawase	800
raamen	500
tempura soba	750
koohii	300
koora	300
juusu	300
biiru	500
sooda	300

You: _____ 1

Waiter: _____ 2

You: _____ 3

Waiter: _____ 4

You: _____ 5

Waiter: _____ 6

You: _____ 7

Waiter: _____ 8

Talking About Daily Activities

A. Answer the following questions regarding your own daily schedule.

1. Maiasa nan-ji ni okimasu ka.

   _____

2. Maiasa jogingu o shimasu ka.

   _____

3. Maiasa asagohan o tabemasu ka.

   _____

4. Nan-ji ni gakkoo e ikimasu ka.

   _____

5. Mainichi hirugohan o tabemasu ka.

   _____

6. Mainichi jugyoo ni demasu ka.

   _____

7. Mainichi juusu o nomimasu ka.

   _____

8. Mainichi toshokan e ikimasu ka.

   _____

9. Mainichi terebi o mimasu ka.

   _____

10 Mainichi undoo o shimasu ka.

   _____

11. Mainichi hon o yomimasu ka.

   _____

12. Nan-ji ni benkyoo shimasu ka.

   _____

13. Doko de benkyoo shimasu ka.

   _____

14. Mainichi nani-ji ni nemasu ka.

   _____

B. Here are ten statements about John Kawamura's typical day. Mark each one as either true (T) or false (F), basing your answers on Kawamura's schedule as given in Activity 5, p. 41, of the main textbook.

1. _____ Gozen juuni-ji ni nemasu.

2. _____ Gogo san-ji ni koohii o nomimasu.

3. _____ Gogo hachi-ji ni bangohan o tabemasu.

4. _____ Gogo ichi-ji ni hirugohan o tabemasu.

5. _____ Gozen ku-ji ni gakkoo e ikimasu.

6. _____ Gozen shichi-ji ni okimasu.

7. _____ Gogo ni-ji ni terebi o mimasu.

C. Complete the following dialogues, basing your answers on Kawamura's schedule in Activity 5 of the main textbook.

1. A: Kawamura-san wa nan-ji ni asagohan o tabemasu ka.

   B: _____1 ni tabemasu.

   A: Nani o tabemasu ka.

   B: Toosuto o _____2.

2. A: Kawamura-san wa mainichi terebi _____1 mimasu ka.

   B: Hai, mimasu.

   A: Nan-ji ni terebi o _____2 ka.

   B: _____3 ni terebi o mimasu.

3. A: Kawamura-san wa _____1 ni gakkoo e ikimasu ka.

   B: _____2 ni gakkoo _____3 ikimasu.

4. A: Kawamura-san wa gozen hachi-ji goro doko e ikimasu ka.

   B: _____ e ikimasu.

5. A: Kawamura-san wa gozen juuni-ji _____1 nani o shimasu ka.

   B: _____2.

D. Answer each of the following questions by telling if and how often you do the activities asked about.

USEFUL VOCABULARY

tokidoki	*sometimes*
Amari shimasen.	*I don't do it very often.*
Amari ikimasen.	*I don't go very often.*
Zenzen shimasen.	*I don't do it at all.*
Zenzen ikimasen.	*I don't go at all.*

1. Asagohan o tabemasu ka.

   _____

2. Gakkoo e ikimasu ka.

   _____

3. Jugyoo ni demasu ka.

   _____

4. Hirugohan o tabemasu ka.

_____

5. Hon o yomimasu ka.

_____

6. Koohii o nomimasu ka.

_____

7. Toshokan e ikimasu ka.

_____

8. Terebi o mimasu ka.

_____

9. Ongaku o kikimasu ka.

_____

10. Benkyoo shimasu ka.

_____

11. Tegami o kakimasu ka.

_____

12. Deeto shimasu ka.

_____

13. Kaimono ni ikimasu ka.

_____

14. Tomodachi ni aimasu ka.

_____

15. Nihongo o renshuu shimasu ka.

_____

E. Match each clock with the time expression it represents.

1. _____ san-ji juugo-hun

2. _____ yo-ji nijuugo-hun

3. _____ ku-ji go-hun

4. _____ shichi-ji gojuugo-hun

5. _____ juuni-ji yonjuugo-hun

6. _____ juuichi-ji sanjuugo-hun

7. _____ ichi-ji han

F. Write up your own daily schedule in Japanese. If it's not the same every day, choose one day of the week. Write *at least* seven sentences.

1. _____

2. _____

3. _____

4. _____

5. _____

6. _____

7. _____

Japanese Writing Systems

Now that you've learned hiragana and katakana, you can practice writing complete sentences. Transcribe the following sentences into hiragana. Particles you have to watch for are underlined.

1. Kyoo wa kin-yoobi desu ka. (Is today Friday?)

   _____

2. Juu-ji ni gakkoo e kimashita. (I came to school at ten.)

   _____

3. Nihongo o benkyoo shimashita. (I studied Japanese.)

   _____

4. Kore wa kyookasho desu. (This is a textbook.)

   _____

5. Watashi wa Yamada-san to issho ni Sano-san no uchi e ikimashita.
   (I went to Mr. Sano's house with Mr. Yamada.)

   _____

6. Yuugohan ni niku o tabemashita. (I ate meat for dinner.)

   _____

Now, watch out for katakana words, too!

7. Kinoo Rosanzerusu <u>e</u> ikimashita. (I went to Los Angeles yesterday.)

_____

8. Terebi de myuujikku shoo <u>o</u> mimashita. (I watched a musical show on TV.)

_____

9. Senshuu Chappurin no eega <u>o</u> mimashita. (I saw a [Charlie] Chaplin movie last week.)

_____

10. Satoo-san <u>wa</u> kafeteria <u>e</u> itte, remoneedo <u>o</u> nomimashita.
    (Mr. Sato went to the cafeteria and drank lemonade.)

_____

11. Supagetti <u>wa</u> arimasu ka. (Do you have spaghetti?)

_____

12. Buraun-san <u>wa</u> fisshu baagaa <u>o</u> tabemashita. (Mr. Brown ate a fish burger.)

_____

13. Depaato de aoi shatsu <u>o</u> kaimashita. (I bought a blue shirt at the department store.)

_____

14. Kyoo <u>wa</u> basu de gakkoo <u>e</u> kimashita. (I came to school by bus today.)

_____

15. Kawamura-san wa mainichi imooto to jogingu o shimasu.
    (Mr. Kawamura jogs with his sister every day.)

_____

CHAPTER 1

クラスメート

Listening Comprehension Activities

Nationalities and Languages

A. Listen as Cody Smith tells Kunio Satoo about his roommate. Then complete the Japanese summary by filling in the blanks.

コロナドさんはスミスさんの_____です。アメリカ人_____。コロナ

ドさんはメキシコの_____です。メキシコ人は_____を話します。

B. Listen as Smith tells Satoo about his Japanese class. Then complete the English summary by filling in the blanks.

USEFUL VOCABULARY
もちろん   of course

In Smith's _____ class, there are about _____ students. There are

some _____, _____, _____, and

_____ students and one student from _____. Smith speaks

_____ with his classmates.

C. Listen to the passage about Maria Nakajima, and find out what language(s) each member of her family speaks. Then complete the following sentences by filling in the names of the appropriate languages.

USEFUL VOCABULARY
じょうず (な)   good at
いっしょに   together
たいへん (な)   troublesome
おとうさん   father
おかあさん   mother
ごりょうしん   parents

1. Maria speaks _____.

2. Maria's father speaks _____.

3. Maria's mother speaks _____.

4. Maria's parents speak _____ with each other.

5. Three of them speak _____ together.

Personal Information

A. Listen as four students introduce themselves. Then complete each of the following sentences by writing in the initials of the person best described by the statement.
(LJ: Lois Johnson   PY: Peggy Yu   SL: Susana Lopez   JW: Julie Wilson)

Example: <u>LJ</u> is from New York.

USEFUL VOCABULARY

まだ   not . . . yet (neg)

1. _____ is majoring in mathematics.

2. _____ is a freshman.

3. _____ is studying American Literature.

4. _____ does not have a major yet.

5. _____ is a graduate student.

6. _____ speaks Spanish.

7. _____ is studying economics.

8. _____ is a senior.

9. _____ is from China.

10. _____ is English.

B. Listen as Midori Momoi tells Kunio Satoo about her living arrangements. Then determine whether each of the following statements is true (T) or false (F).

1. _____ Midori lives in a university dorm.

2. _____ She has three roommates.

3. _____ Her roommates are all Korean.

4. _____ They all go to the same university.

5. _____ Two of her roommates are freshmen, but they are fluent in Japanese.

C. The interviewer is asking two different students, A and B, about their lives. You will hear each question twice. Write the letter of the best answer in the blank corresponding to the question.

A	B
a. 224-5679 です。	a. 六月生まれです。
b. こう学です。	b. とうきょうです。
c. ユーです。	c. 二十さいです。
d. ちゅうごくです。	d. めいじ大学です。

A: 1._____   2._____   3._____   4._____

B: 1._____   2._____   3._____   4._____

D. Listen to the conversation between Lin and Nakajima. Then determine whether each of the following statements is true (T) or false (F).

USEFUL VOCABULARY

ほんとう   true

1. _____ Nakajima and Lin have met each other before.

2. _____ Lin is from Ann Arbor.

3. _____ They are both students.

4. _____ They belong to the same department.

5. _____ Professor Thomas teaches history.

E. Listen to the conversation between Professor Arai and three students. Then fill in the blanks with the initial of the person best described by each sentence.

S: Smith   Y: Yu   K: Kraus   A: Professor Arai

EXAMPLE: __A__ notices what time it is.

1. _____ was born in June.

2. _____ is 24 years old.

3. _____ is 27 years old.

4. _____ was born in December.

5. _____ is 20 years old.

6. _____ and _____ were born in September.

7. _____ does not like to discuss age.

Around Campus

A. Listen as Professor Arai gives a dictation to her class. Then look at the following list, and circle the items she mentions during the dictation.

chalk   blackboard   desk   chair   notebook   textbook   pen

B. You will hear two descriptions, one of Professor Saitoo's office and one of the Japanese classroom. Complete the following statements by filling in *S* for Professor Saitoo's office or *J* for the Japanese classroom.

USEFUL VOCABULARY

ちかい   *near*
とおい   *far*

1. _____ is on the third floor.

2. _____ is far from the library.

3. _____ is used on Mondays and Wednesdays.

4. _____ is on the first floor.

5. _____ is in the Sociology Department Building.

6. _____ is near the cafeteria.

7. _____ 's room number is 164.

8. _____ 's phone number is 227-2813.

C. Listen to the following conversation between Smith and Satoo. Then complete the English summary by filling in the blanks.

USEFUL VOCABULARY

りっぱ（な）   *splendid-looking*
よく   *often*

Smith and Satoo are looking at the _____, which is a splendid-looking building. There is a

_____ in the building. _____ often goes there. Both Satoo and Smith like

_____, so they decide to go there on _____.

D. Listen to the description of Professor Arai's daily routine. Then answer the following questions about it in English.

USEFUL VOCABULARY

かいぎ meeting
やすみ rest, time off

1. Where is Professor Arai's office?

_____

2. What is her phone number?

_____

3. When does her Japanese class meet?

_____

4. When does she have her office hours?

_____

5. What does she have on Tuesdays?

_____

6. Where does she spend her weekends?

_____

7. What does she do on weekends?

_____

E. You will hear ten statements. Match each statement with the question it could serve as an answer for. The first five statements will match up with the first five questions, and the second set of five statements will match up with the second set of five questions.

USEFUL VOCABULARY

くるま car

1. _____ あれはだれですか。
2. _____ それはどこですか。
3. _____ クラスは何じからですか。
4. _____ あれはだれのくるまですか。
5. _____ しゅっしんはどこですか。
6. _____ これはいくらですか。
7. _____ あの人はどなたですか。
8. _____ これは何の本ですか。
9. _____ どこへいきますか。
10. _____ 日本語のクラスはいつですか。

F. Midori Momoi and Lois Johnson had a party at their place last night. Listen as they clean up the next morning. Then look over the list of items, circling the items they have found and crossing out the items that are missing.

camera   sweater   umbrella   watch   bag   shoes

G. A lot of things have accumulated in the East Asian Language Department's lost and found collection, and Professor Arai has decided to try to find the rightful owners. Listen as she asks her students about the various objects, and then match each object with its owner.

1. ____ umbrella

2. ____ dictionary

3. ____ bag

4. ____ fountain pen

5. ____ magazine

6. ____ textbook

a. Kraus
b. Smith
c. Scott
d. Kim
e. Johnson
f. Yu

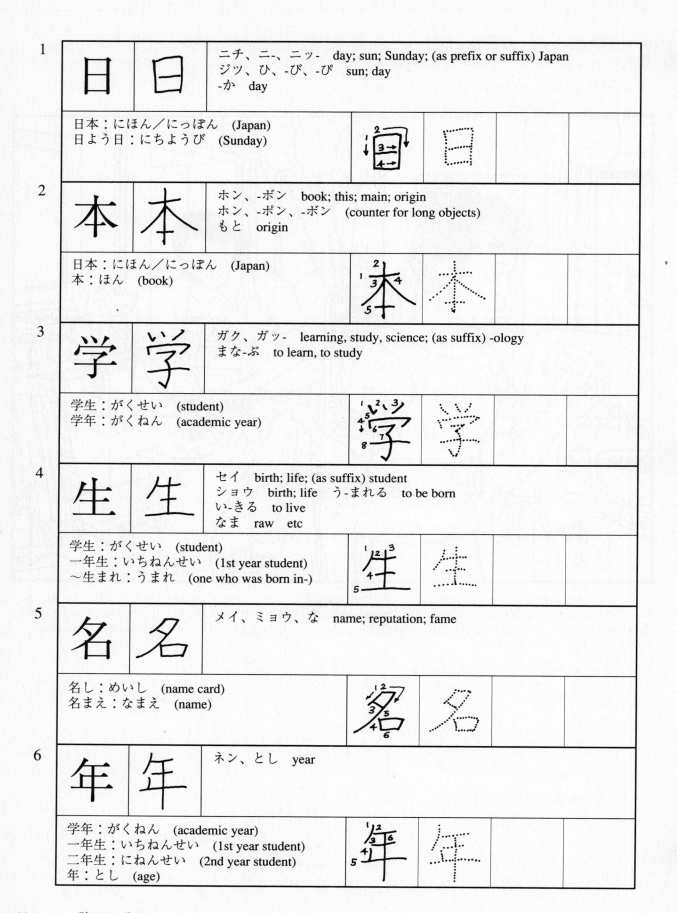

1	日 日	ニチ、ニ-、ニッ- day; sun; Sunday; (as prefix or suffix) Japan ジツ、ひ、-び、-ぴ sun; day -か day				
	日本：にほん／にっぽん (Japan) 日よう日：にちようび (Sunday)					

2	本 本	ホン、-ボン book; this; main; origin ホン、-ポン、-ボン (counter for long objects) もと origin				
	日本：にほん／にっぽん (Japan) 本：ほん (book)					

3	学 学	ガク、ガッ- learning, study, science; (as suffix) -ology まな-ぶ to learn, to study				
	学生：がくせい (student) 学年：がくねん (academic year)					

4	生 生	セイ birth; life; (as suffix) student ショウ birth; life う-まれる to be born い-きる to live なま raw etc				
	学生：がくせい (student) 一年生：いちねんせい (1st year student) ～生まれ：うまれ (one who was born in-)					

5	名 名	メイ、ミョウ、な name; reputation; fame				
	名し：めいし (name card) 名まえ：なまえ (name)					

6	年 年	ネン、とし year				
	学年：がくねん (academic year) 一年生：いちねんせい (1st year student) 二年生：にねんせい (2nd year student) 年：とし (age)					

7	何 何	カ、なに、なん-　what

何：なに　(what) 何ご：なにご　(what language) 何ですか：なんですか　(what is it?) 何年生：なんねんせい　(what year student)	何	何		

8	月 月	ゲツ、ゲッ-　moon; month; Monday ガツ、ガッ-　month つき　moon; month

月よう日：げつようび　(Monday) 何月生まれ：なんがつうまれ　(What month 　　were you born in?) 一月：いちがつ　(January)	月	月		

9	人 人	ジン、ニン、ひと、-びと　man; person; human being

日本人：にほんじん　(a Japanese) アメリカ人：あめりかじん　(an American) この人：このひと　(this person)	人	人		

10	一 一	イチ、イツ、イッ-、ひと-つ、ひと-　one; a

一月：いちがつ　(January) 一年生：いちねんせい　(1st year student) 一さい：いっさい　(one year old) 一つ：ひとつ　(one year old / one item)	一	………		

11	二 二	ニ、ふた-つ、ふた-　two

二月：にがつ　(February) 二年生：にねんせい　(2nd year student) 二つ：ふたつ　(two years old / two items)	二	二		

12	三 三	サン、みっ-つ、み-、み-つ　three

三月：さんがつ　(March) 三年生：さんねんせい　(3rd year student) 三つ：みっつ　(three years old / three items)	三	三		

13	四 四	シ、よっ-つ、よ-、よん、よ-つ　four

四月：しがつ　(April)
四年生：よねんせい　(4th year student)
四さい：よんさい　(four years old)
四つ：よっつ　(four years old / four items)

14	五 五	ゴ、いつ-つ、いつ-　five

五月：ごがつ　(May)
五さい：ごさい　(five years old)
五つ：いつつ　(five years old / five items)

15	六 六	ロク、ロッ-、リク、むっ-つ、む、む-つ、むい　six

六月：ろくがつ　(June)
六さい：ろくさい　(six years old)
六つ：むっつ　(six years old / six items)
六かい：ろっかい　(sixth floor)

16	七 七	シチ、なな-つ、なな、なの-　seven

七月：しちがつ　(July)
七さい：ななさい　(seven years old)
七つ：ななつ　(seven years old / seven items)

17	八 八	ハチ、ハッ-、やっ-つ、や、や-つ、よう-　eight

八月：はちがつ　(August)
八さい：はっさい　(eight years old)
八つ：やっつ　(eight years old / eight items)
八かい：はっかい　(eight floor)

18	九 九	ク、キュウ、ここの-つ、ここの-　nine

九月：くがつ　(September)
九さい：きゅうさい　(nine years old)
九つ：ここのつ　(nine years old / nine items)
九じ：くじ　(nine o'clock)

19	十	十	ジュウ、ジッ、ジュッ、とお、と- ten		
	十月：じゅうがつ　(October) 十さい：じゅっさい／じっさい　(ten years old) 十：とお／じゅう　(ten years old / ten items) 十かい：じゅっかい／じっかい　(tenth floor)		十	十	
20	百	百	ヒャク、ヒャッ-、-ビャク、-ピャク、もも　hundred; many		
	百さい：ひゃくさい　(100 years old) 三百：さんびゃく　(three hundred) 六百：ろっぴゃく　(six hundred) 八百：はっぴゃく　(eight hundred)		百	百	
21	先	先	セン、さき　earlier; ahead; priority; future; destination; the tip		
	先生：せんせい　(teacher)		先	先	
22	話	話	ワ、はなし　conversation, story はな-す　speak		
	話します：はなします　((will) speak)		話	話	
23	語	語	ゴ　word かた-る　talk, relate かた-らう　converse		
	日本語：にほんご　(Japanese language) えい語：えいご　(English language) スペイン語：すぺいんご　(Spanish language) 何語：なにご　(what language)		語	語	
24	大	大	ダイ　big, large, great; (short for 大学, university); (as suffix) the size of... タイ、おお-きい、おお-　big, large, greeat おお-いに　very much, greatly		
	大学：だいがく　(university) 大学生：だいがくせい　(university student) 大すきです：だいすきです　(I like it very much) 大きい：おおきい　(big)		大	大	

KANJI EXERCISES (1)

1. Match each kanji or kanji compound with its closest English equivalent.

1. 日本
   _____

2. 何
   _____

3. 五十九
   _____

4. 学生
   _____

5. 名
   _____

6. 四月生まれ
   _____

7. 人
   _____

8. 百
   _____

9. 一年生
   _____

10. 学年
    _____

11. 本
    _____

12. 月よう日
    _____

13. 七さい
    _____

14. 十八
    _____

15. 日本人
    _____

16. 日本語
    _____

17. 話
    _____

18. 大
    _____

19. 先生
    _____

(a) freshman/first year student
(b) seven years old
(c) person
(d) hundred
(e) book
(f) Japanese person
(g) fifty-nine
(h) name
(i) academic year
(j) what
(k) Monday
(l) Sunday
(m) sixteen
(n) eighteen
(o) eighty
(p) Japan
(q) to speak
(r) student
(s) teacher
(t) Japanese language
(u) one who was born in April
(v) big

2. Write hurigana for each kanji or kanji compound. Pay special attention to the changes in pronunciation that may occur when kanji are compounded.

1. 何月生まれ	2. 名まえ	3. 九月
_____	_____	_____
4. 日本人	5. 八さい	6. 学生
_____	_____	_____
7. 月よう日	8. 百さい	9. 大きい
_____	_____	_____
10. 四月	11. 一年生	12. 日よう日
_____	_____	_____
13. 四さい	14. 六月	15. 一さい
_____	_____	_____
16. 三つ	17. 五つ	18. 十二月
_____	_____	_____
19. 九さい	20. 話します	21. 何語
_____	_____	_____
22. 四年生	23. 大学	24. 先生
_____	_____	_____

3. Fill in the blank with the kanji for the word or phrase that is spelled out in hiragana under the line.

1. わたしは、_____ ではありません。
　　　　　　　　　にほんじん

2. _____ ですか。
　　なんねんせい

3. お _____ 1 まえは _____ 2 ですか。
　　　　　な　　　　　　　　　　なん

4. わたしは、_____ _____ まれです。
　　　　　　　　ごがつ　　　　　　　　　　う

5. カワムラさんは、_____ 1 です。
　　　　　　　　　　がくせい

　　たなかさんは、_____ 2 です。
　　　　　　　　せんせい

6. これは、だれの _____ ですか。
　　　　　　　　　ほん

7. コンピュータのクラスは _____ 1 よう _____ 2 です。
　　　　　　　　　　　げつ　　　　　　　　　　　び

8. チンさんは、_____ 1 を _____ 2 しますか。
　　　　　　　なにご　　　　　　　　　はな

4. Write the kanji for the numbers one to ten and for the number one hundred in order.

1. _____   100. _____

2. _____

3. _____

4. _____

5. _____

6. _____

7. _____

8. _____

9. _____

10. _____

Writing Activities

Nationalities and Languages

Fill in the parentheses with the name of the language or languages spoken by each group of people. If you don't know, look up the information in an encyclopedia or world almanac.

EXAMPLE:　日本人は (日本語) を話します。

1.　アメリカ人は (_____) を話します。

2.　メキシコ人は (_____) を話します。

3.　カナダ人は (_____) を話します。

4.　イギリス人は (_____) を話します。

5.　ちゅうごく人は (_____) を話します。

6.　ブラジル人は (_____) を話します。

7.　アルゼンチン人は (_____) を話します。

Personal Information

A. The lefthand column is a list of academic subjects. The righthand column is a list of words or expressions associated with these subjects. Match the items by writing the appropriate letter in the parentheses between the columns.

1.　すう学　　　　(___)　　a.　クラシック
　　　　　　　　　　　　　　b.　スペイン語
2.　けいざい学　 (___)　　c.　ヘミングウェイ
3.　おんがく　　 (___)　　d.　$3(27 \div 54) / 4 = ?$
4.　か学　　　　 (___)　　e.　マルクス
　　　　　　　　　　　　　　f.　H_2O, CO_2
5.　ぶん学　　　 (___)

6.　がいこく語　 (___)

B. Read the five self-introductions below and try to figure out which country each person comes from. If you aren't sure, check a world almanac or atlas to see if you have guessed correctly. Then write in the names of the countries in the blanks below.

a.　わたしはホセ・ガルシアです。しゅっしんはアカプルコです。スペイン語を話します。
b.　わたしはパウロ・イソベです。みなみアメリカのしゅっしんです。ポルトガル語を話します。日本語 もちょっと話します。
c.　わたしはキャシー・マイヤーです。フランス語もえい語も話します。うちはケベックです。
d.　わたしはポーン・サナサフォーンです。タイ語とフランス語を話します。しゅっしんはチェンマイです。
e.　わたしはジャミラ・サイードです。フランス語とアラビア語を話します。しゅっしんはアフリカです。 わたしのくにはスペインにとてもちかいです。

Answers:　a. _____　b. _____　c. _____

　　　　　　d. _____　e. _____

C. Match each question in the lefthand column with the most appropriate response in the righthand column.

1. _____ お名まえは。
2. _____ しゅっしんはどこですか。
3. _____ おくにはどちらですか。
4. _____ おすまいはどこですか。
5. _____ おいくつですか。
6. _____ おでんわばんごうは。
7. _____ 何月生まれですか。
8. _____ せんこうは何ですか。
9. _____ 何年生ですか。

a. ボストンです。
b. アメリカです。
c. たなかです。
d. 12月生まれです。
e. 1年生です。
f. 大学のりょうです。
g. 21さいです。
h. コンピュータサイエンスです。
i. 03-456-9872です。

D. Here is a list of five of John Kawamura's friends from his Japanese class. Write a brief paragraph about each of them, using all the personal information in the chart.

Name	hometown	year	age	birth mo.	major	languages
1. Kim （キム）	Seoul, Korea （ソウル）	soph.	20	May	economics	Korean
2. Vogel （フォーゲル）	Geneva, Switzerland （ジェネーブ、スイス）	jr.	22	April	engineering	German, French
3. Lim （リム）	Kota Boru, Malaysia （コタバル、マレーシア）	jr.	23	July	sociology	English, Chinese Malay（マライ語）
4. Perez （ペレス）	Dallas, Texas （ダラス、テキサス）	fresh.	18	October	math	English, Spanish
5. Cohen （コーエン）	Des Moines, Iowa （デモイン、アイオワ）	grad.	28	Sept.	history	English

1. _____

_____

_____

2. _____

_____

_____

3. _____

_____

_____

4. _____

_____

_____

5. _____

_____

_____

E. Now write paragraphs about two of your own friends, following the same format as exercise D.

1. _____

_____

_____

2. _____

_____

_____

Around Campus

A. Complete the following conversations, using the information contained in this directory of a campus building.

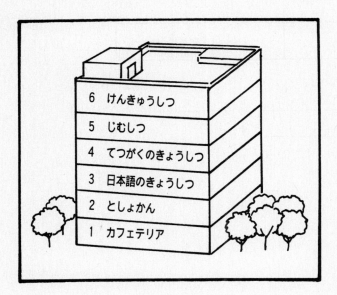

1. A: すみません。としょかんはどこですか。

B: あのビルの _____ かいです。

2. A: すみません。日本語のきょうしつはどこですか。

B: あのビルの _____ かいです。

3. A: ＿＿＿＿＿＿＿＿＿＿。　じむしつはどこですか。

   B: あのビルの ＿＿＿＿＿＿＿＿＿＿ かいです。

4. A: すみません。＿＿＿＿＿＿＿＿＿＿ はどこですか。

   B: あのビルの１かいです。

5. A: ＿＿＿＿＿＿＿＿＿＿。＿＿＿＿＿＿＿＿＿＿ はどこですか。

   B: あのビルの５かいです。

B. Look over this student's weekly schedule. Then fill in the blanks in the Japanese statements with the appropriate days of the week.

	Sun	Mon	Tue	Wed	Thurs	Fri	Sat
9:00		French		French		French	
10:00			history		history		
11:00		political science		law		economics	
12:00							
1:00							
2:00							

1. フランス語のクラスは ＿＿＿＿＿＿＿＿＿＿ と ＿＿＿＿＿＿＿＿＿＿ と ＿＿＿＿＿＿＿＿＿＿ です。

2. れきし学のクラスは ＿＿＿＿＿＿＿＿＿＿ と ＿＿＿＿＿＿＿＿＿＿ です。

3. けいざい学のクラスは ＿＿＿＿＿＿＿＿＿＿ です。

4. せいじ学のクラスは ＿＿＿＿＿＿＿＿＿＿ です。

5. ほう学のクラスは ＿＿＿＿＿＿＿＿＿＿ です。

Name _____ Date _____ Class _____

C. This was Linda Brown's weekly class schedule the semester before she came to Japan. Read over the schedule and answer the questions below in Japanese.

Linda Brown's Schedule

Time	Mon	Tue	Wed	Thurs	Fri
8:00		Japanese history		Japanese history	
9:00					
10:00	Japanese	Japanese	Japanese	Japanese	Japanese
11:00					
12:00	Chinese history		Chinese history		Chinese history
1:00		Japanese literature		Japanese literature	
2:00					
3:00	Tennis		Tennis		Tennis
4:00					

a. ブラウンさんの日本のれきしのクラスは何よう日の何じですか。

_____

b. ちゅうごくのれきしのクラスもそうですか。

_____

c. 日本語は11じですか。何よう日ですか。

_____

d. ほかに (*other than that*)、ブラウンさんは何をべんきょうしています (*is studying*) か。

_____

e. それは何よう日の何じですか。

_____

f. ブラウンさんのせんこうは何ですか。 (Write your guess.)

_____

D. Choose five current television programs and write two or three sentences about each of them, including the day of the week and time they are on, what kinds of programs they are, and, if you can, a statement about whether you like or dislike each program or the people featured on it.

The following words may come in handy:

ばんぐみ (program)	クイズばんぐみ	ドラマ
メロドラマ	ドキュメンタリー	サスペンス
ニュース	ミステリー	スポーツ
コメディー	えいが (movie)	インタビューばんぐみ (talk show)

1. _____

   _____

   _____

2. _____

   _____

   _____

3. _____

   _____

   _____

4. _____

   _____

   _____

5. _____

   _____

   _____

E. Fill in the blanks and complete the conversation.

A: これは、だれ＿＿＿＿＿＿＿ しゃしんですか。

B: それ＿＿＿＿＿＿、わたし＿＿＿＿＿＿ しゃしんです。

A: この人＿＿＿＿＿＿、だれですか。

B: その人＿＿＿＿＿＿、まちださん＿＿＿＿＿＿。

A: まちださん＿＿＿＿＿＿日本人です＿＿＿＿＿＿。

B: はい、日本人＿＿＿＿＿＿。

A: まちださん＿＿＿＿＿＿、大学＿＿＿＿＿＿先生です＿＿＿＿＿＿。

B: いいえ、先生＿＿＿＿＿＿ありません。学生＿＿＿＿＿＿。

A: まちださん＿＿＿＿＿＿せんこう＿＿＿＿＿＿何ですか。

B: 日本ぶん学です。

A: そうですか。わたし＿＿＿＿＿＿せんこう＿＿＿＿＿＿日本ぶんがくです。

B: そうですか。

F. Using these question words, make up questions which would yield the following answers, and write them in the blanks marked "A."

何　だれ／どなた　いつ　どこ　何さい　いくら

1. A: _____

   B: それはコンピュータです。

2. A: _____

   B: あのビルの3かいです。

3. A: _____

   B: おおの先生です。

4. A: _____

   B: 日よう日にテニスをします。

5. A: _____

   B: 2000えんです。

6. A: _____

   B: 30さいです。

7. A: _____

   B: とうきょうのしゅっしんです。

8. A: _____

   B: それはブラウンさんのテレビです。

9. A: _____

   B: わたしのせんこうは、しゃかい学です。

10. A: _____

   B: それは、か学の本です。

G. You have just arrived at the Japanese university where you will be studying for a year. The international students' office has introduced you to a Japanese student so you can ask whatever questions you have concerning the university. Now both of you are standing at the entrance to the campus. Try asking the Japanese student the following questions. Then, if you have other questions of your own, ask them, too.

1. You'd like to know what that building is. _____

   _____

2. Point to a statue and find out who it is. _____

   _____

3. Ask who your Japanese teacher is. _____

   _____

4. Find out how old your Japanese teacher is. _____

   _____

5. You'd like to know where students eat lunch. _____

_____

6. Find out how much lunches at the cafeteria cost. _____

_____

7. You'd like to know what time classes start in the morning. _____

_____

8. Ask in which building Japanese classes are held. _____

_____

9. Ask which direction the library is. _____

_____

10. Find out what students do on Saturday afternoons. _____

_____

11. Your own questions: _____

_____

H. You would like to find a Japanese pen pal, so you write up an advertisement to send to a popular Japanese magazine. Include the following information:

1. Your name.
2. Your age.
3. The name of your school and where it is located.
4. What year you are in school.
5. Your major.
6. Where you are from.
7. What languages you speak.
8. Your likes and dislikes.
9. What kind of person you would like to write to.

USEFUL VOCABULARY:

...をさがしています   *I am looking for...*

Begin your advertisement in the following way:

ペンパルをさがしています。 _____

_____

_____

_____

_____

_____

CHAPTER **2**

わたしの町

Listening Comprehension Activities

Commuting

A. John Kawamura is considering moving to a new apartment, so he goes around looking at various possibilities. Listen to the conversation he has with the manager of one apartment building. Then complete the English summary by filling in the blanks.

USEFUL VOCABULARY

あるいて   on foot

Kawamura wonders whether the apartment is _____. The manager tells him that it is

_____ minutes by _____ and _____ minutes on foot.

The next thing Kawamura asks is whether there is a _____ nearby. There is, and it is only

_____ minutes away on foot. The _____, which is only

_____ minutes away, is even closer. The manager tells Kawamura that the apartment is really

very convenient, because among other things, it is also very close to a _____ and a

_____.

B. Listen as Antonio Coronado talks about his home in Mexico and the transportation facilities that serve it. Complete the English summary by filling in the blanks.

Coronado says his home in Mexico is far from everything: in order to go to the university, he has to

_____ to the bus stop, which will take ten minutes; then he has to ride the bus for

_____ minutes to the _____, and from there he has to ride the

_____ for another twenty-five minutes. So altogether, it takes Antonio

_____ minutes to go to the university. _____ and

_____ are also far from home, so his mother sometimes goes shopping by _____

_____ while Antonio goes by _____.

Cities and Neighborhoods

A. You will hear descriptions of the cities of Kyoto and Sapporo. Choose the words that describe each city from the list below.

1. Kyoto: _____

2. Sapporo: _____

a. big   b. old   c. new   d. beautiful   e. a big population   f. quiet   g. quiet in the suburbs
h. interesting buildings   i. famous   j. close to the sea and mountains

B. Listen as Kunio Satoo asks Antonio Coronado about his home in Mexico. Then mark each statement either true (T) or false (F).

1. _____ Coronado comes from a small village near Mexico City.

2. _____ There is a train between the capital and Coronado's village.

3. _____ Coronado likes his village because it is quiet.

4. _____ He does not like the town he lives in now because it is too noisy.

5. _____ Coronado and Satoo live in a college town.

C. Listen as Smith tells Satoo about his Japanese instructor. Then mark each statement either true (T) or false (F).

1. _____ Smith's Japanese instructor is strict.

2. _____ She is a good teacher.

3. _____ The classes are interesting.

4. _____ The classes are long.

5. _____ The exams are hard.

6. _____ The students like their instructor a lot.

7. _____ All the students are easy-going.

Buildings and Places Around Town

A. Listen as Machida tells Brown about her home neighborhood. Then write down five things that are near Machida's house.

USEFUL VOCABULARY

もんだい　　　problem

1. _____   2. _____   3. _____   4. _____   5. _____

B. Listen as a passerby asks Machida for directions to the department store and the bank. Then write in *D* after the phrases that describe the department store and *B* after the phrases that describe the bank.

1. In front of the train station: ____

2. A tall building: ____

3. A small building: ____

4. Near the station: ____

5. A white building: ____

6. Between a coffee shop and a bookstore: ____

C. Listen to the following description of a neighborhood. Then show the location of each building listed by writing its number in the appropriate blank space on the map.

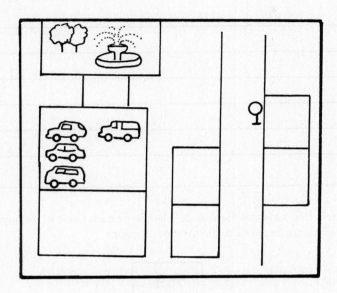

1. my house   2. coffee shop   3. game center   4. supermarket   5. post office   6. sushi shop

D. Listen to the description of a student's room and answer the questions. Give as much information as possible.

USEFUL VOCABULARY

本だな   bookshelf

1. On which side of the room is the window?

_____

2. What is in front of the window?

_____

3. What is on the right side of the desk? On the left side?

_____

4. Where is the TV?

_____

5. Where is the bag?

_____

6. What is inside the bag?

_____

E. Listen to the description of the Green Building, and then indicate on the drawing what is located on each floor.

USEFUL VOCABULARY

ちか   underground, basement

6	
5	
4	
3	
2	
1	
B₁	

F. Listen as Professor Arai tells her students where to sit. Then write each name in the appropriate position on the seating chart. The top of the chart corresponds to the front of the room.

	先生	
	コロナド	

Counting

A. Machida is stopped in front of a department store by a man who claims to be a policeman. Listen as the man orders her to show him the contents of her purse. Then indicate the quantity of each item he finds in her purse.

USEFUL VOCABULARY

けいかん   *policeman*
…をあけてください。   *Please open...*

EXAMPLE: camera _____one_____

1. credit cards _____

2. pens _____

3. wallets _____

4. money _____

5. books _____

6. film _____

7. photographs _____

B. Listen to Maria Nakajima talk about her roommate Martha. Then list the things that each of them has.

    USEFUL VOCABULARY

    かねもち（の）   *rich*
    びんぼう（な）   *poor*
    ねこ   *cat*

1. Maria has _____

2. Martha has _____

C. Listen as Masaru Honda interviews the entertainer Himiko. Then complete the English summary by filling in the blanks.

    USEFUL VOCABULARY

    しょくじ   *meal*
    コック   *cook*
    りょうり   *dish, cuisine*

Himiko has _____ houses. In the house in Azabu, there are _____ rooms, _____ pools, and _____ restaurants where she has cooks and _____ waiters.

D. Listen as Brown talks about the students in Professor Yokoi's class and write down the number of the students who :

1. don't like Professor Yokoi: _____

2. don't like homework: _____

3. like homework: _____

4. like kanji: _____

5. like Japanese food: _____

6. don't like sushi: _____

7. like Tokyo: _____

8. don't like the Japanese class: _____

1	間　間	カン　interval; space; between; (as suffix) between, among あいだ　interval (of space or time); between, among ま　space, room; pause; a rest (in music); time; leisure; luck etc.			
	一時間：いちじかん　(one hours) ＡとＢの間：ＡとＢのあいだ (between A and B)	間	間		
2	半　半	ハン、-バン　half, semi-; odd number なか-ば　half, semi-; middle, halfway; partly			
	一時間半：いちじかんはん (one hour and a half) 四時間半：よじかんはん　(four hours and a half) 九時半：くじはん　(9:30)	半	半		
3	上　上	ジョウ　upper, top, above, first volume / part (of a series); top-grade, etc. うえ　up, upper part, top, above, over, besides, on top of, upon, etc. あ-げる　to raise, to lift up, give　あ-がる　to rise; to go / come etc			
	上：うえ　(upper part) 本の上：ほんのうえ　(on the book)	上	上		
4	下　下	カ、ゲ　low, lower; below, under／した　lower part, below, under さ-げる　to hang, to suspend, to lower／さ-がる　to hand down, to fall, to go / come down; to step back／くだ-る　to come / go / get / step down; to be given; to be less than／くだ-さる　to bestow etc			
	下：した　(lower part) テレビの下：てれびのした　(under the TV) ち下てつ：ちかてつ　(subway)	下	下		
5	分　分	フン、-プン　(of time / arc) ブン　portion　ブ　portion, 1 percent わ-ける／かつ　divide, share, distinguish　わ-かれる　be separated わ-かる　understand			
	一分：いっぷん　(one minute) 五分：ごふん　(five minutes) 十分：じゅっぷん／じっぷん　(ten minutes) 分かります：わかります　(understand)	分	分		
6	小　小	ショウ、ちい-さい、こ-、お-　little, small			
	小さい：ちいさい　(small) 小さくありません：ちいさくありません 　(is not small)	小	小		

7	好	好	コウ、この-む、す-く、す-き　to like, be fond of …ず-き　lover / fan of... よ-し、い-い、よ-い　good, favorable, alright
	好きです：すきです　((I) like (it)) 大好きです：だいすきです 　((I) like (it) very much)		

8	町	町	チョウ　street, town; (unit of length, about 109 m); (unit of area, 　about 0.992 ha) まち　street, town; quarter
	わたしの町：わたしのまち　(my town) 町田さん：まちださん　(Mr./Ms. Machida)		

9	田	田	デン、た、-だ　rice field, paddy
	山田さん：やまださん　(Mr./Ms. Yamada) 町田さん：まちださん　(Mr./Ms. Machida) 田中さん：たなかさん　(Mr./Ms. Tanaka)		

10	左	左	サ、ひだり　left
	左：ひだり　(left) 山田さんの左：やまださんのひだり 　(the left of Mr./Ms. Yamada)		

11	右	右	ウ、ユウ、みぎ　right
	右：みぎ　(right) 山田さんの右：やまださんのみぎ 　(the right of Mr./Ms. Yamada)		

12	中	中	チュウ　middle; China／-チュウ、-ジュウ　throughout, during, within なか　inside; midst うち　among
	中ごく：ちゅうごく　(China) 中：なか　(inside) 一日中：いちにちじゅう　(all day)		

13	外 外	ガイ outside, external, foreign／ゲ outside, external そと outside, outdoor／ほか other／はず-す to take off, to remove, to disconnect, to miss, etc.／はず-れる to come/slip off, to be/get out of place, to be disconnected, etc.		
	外：そと (outside) レストランの外：れすとらんのそと (outside the restaurant)	外	外	
14	前 前	ゼン、まえ before, front		
	前：まえ (front / before) 名前：なまえ (name) 大学の前：だいがくのまえ (in front of the university)	前	前	
15	後 後	ゴ、のち after, later／コウ、うし-ろ behind あと afterward, subsequent, back retro- おく-れる to be late, to lag behind		
	後ろ：うしろ (behind) たてものの後ろ：たてもののうしろ (behind the building)	後	後	
16	時 時	ジ、とき、-どき time, hour		
	一時間：いちじかん (one hour) 何時ですか：なんじですか (what time is it?)	時	時	
17	山 山	サン、-ザン、やま mountain		
	山：やま 山田さん：やまださん (Mr./Ms. Yamada) 山口さん：やまぐちさん (Mr./Ms. Yamaguchi)	山	山	
18	口 口	コウ、ク、くち、-ぐち mouth		
	口：くち (mouth) 人口：じんこう (population) 山口さん：やまぐちさん (Mr./Ms. Yamaguchi)	口	口	

19	千	千	セン、-ゼン、ち thousand
	千：せん （one thousand） 二千二百：にせんにひゃく 　（two thousand two hundred） 三千：さんぜん （three thousand）		千　千
20	万	万	マン ten thousand, myriad バン countless, myriad, all よろず ten thousand, all sorts of every...
	一万：いちまん （ten thousand） 二千二百万：にせんにひゃくまん 　（twenty-two million）		万　万
21	方	方	ホウ、-ボウ、-ポウ direction, side; way, square かた、-がた direction; person; method
	この方：このかた （this person） あの方：あのかた （that person）		方　方
22	近	近	キン、ちか-い、-ぢか near, close, recent, near future
	近い：ちかい （close） 近じょ：きんじょ （neighborhood）		近　近
23	遠	遠	エン、オン、とお-い、-どお-い far, distant
	遠い：とおい （far）		遠　遠
24	有	有	ユウ、ウ、あ-る be, exist, have
	有名：ゆうめい （famous） 有名な人：ゆうめいなひと （famous person）		有　有

KANJI EXERCISES (2)

1. Match each kanji or kanji compound with its closest English equivalent.

1. 山 _____   2. 千 _____   3. 町 _____

4. 外 _____   5. 口 _____   6. 半 _____

7. 下 _____   8. 間 _____   9. 田 _____

10. 前 _____ 11. 好 _____ 12. 人口 _____

13. 百万 _____ 14. 近 _____ 15. 方 _____

16. 後 _____ 17. 中 _____ 18. 五分 _____

19. 時 _____ 20. 小 _____ 21. 上 _____

22. 右 _____ 23. 二時間 _____ 24. 遠 _____

25. 有名 _____ 26. 左 _____

(a) two hours   (b) between/among   (c) half   (d) upper part   (e) lower part   (f) near
(g) five minutes   (h) small   (i) like   (j) town   (k) rice field   (l) left   (m) right   (n) inside
(o) outside   (p) front   (q) far   (r) behind   (s) time   (t) mountain   (u) mouth   (v) population
(w) thousand   (x) famous   (y) one million   (z) direction/person

2. Write hurigana for each kanji or kanji compound. Pay special attention to the changes in pronunciation that may occur when kanji are compounded.

1. 一時間半 _____   2. としょかんの中 _____

3. テーブルの下 _____   4. 大学の前 _____

5. 日本の人口 _____   6. 山田さんの右 _____

7. えいがかんの後ろ _____   8. 二千二百万人 _____

9. 大きいびょういんの左 _____   10. いえの外 _____

11. スーパーとぎんこうの間 _____   12. つくえの上 _____

13. 大好きです _____   14. 小さい町 _____

15. 近いです _____   16. 遠いです _____

17. 名前 _____   18. 有名です _____

19. 四時五分 _____   20. あの方 (that person) _____

3. Fill in the blanks with the kanji for the words or phrases that are spelled out in hiragana below the lines.

1. わたしのうちは _____¹ から _____² いです。
　　　　　　　　　だいがく　　　　　　　　　　　とお

2. でんしゃで _____ です。
　　　　　　　いちじかんはん

3. _____¹ の _____² は _____³ ですか。
　　にほん　　　　　　じんこう　　　　　　なんにん

4. 一おく _____ ぐらいです。
　　　　にせんにひゃくまんにん

5. _____1 さんは、きょうしつの _____2 にいます。
　　　　やまだ　　　　　　　　　　　　　　　　　　　そと

6. スーパーはえきの _____ にあります。
　　　　　　　　　　　　まえ

7. わたしの _____1 は _____2 さいですが、
　　　　　　まち　　　　　　　　　　ちい

_____3 です。
　　ゆうめい

8. こうえんは、がっこうの _____ ろにあります。
　　　　　　　　　　　　　　うし

9. カワムラさんの _____ にブラウンさんがいます。
　　　　　　　　　　みぎ

10. カワムラさんの _____ にギブソンさんがいます。
　　　　　　　　　　ひだり

11. カワムラさんは、_____1 の _____2 にいます。
　　　　　　　　　　ふたり　　　　　　　あいだ

12. わたしはやさいが _____ きです。
　　　　　　　　　　だいす

13. かばんの _____1 に _____2 があります。
　　　　　　なか　　　　　　　　ほん

14. つくえの _____1 に _____2 きないぬがいます。
　　　　　　した　　　　　　　　おお

15. いすの _____1 に _____2 さなねこがいます。
　　　　　うえ　　　　　　　　ちい

16. いま、_____ です。
　　　　　　ごじごふん

17. あの _____ はどなたですか。
　　　　かた

KANJI NOTE

The Chinese character 々 which is called 同の字点 (どうのじてん), does not have a sound or meaning of its own. Its function is to repeat the preceding character, and its sound is determined by the preceding character, so in effect, it's a sort of ditto mark for kanji. Thus, instead of writing 日日 and 人人, you can write 日々 (ひび: day in and day out) and 人々 (ひとびと: people). The following are some kanji compounds that include 々.

佐々木 (ささき: *a family name*)
月々 (つきづき: *every month*)
個々 (ここ: *each*)
多々 (たた: *many*)
少々 (しょうしょう: *a little*)
時々 (ときどき: *sometimes*)

The stroke order of 々 is as follows:

Not every repeated syllable is written with 々. For the time being, use it only to write words that you have actually seen written in kanji in your main textbook or workbook.

Writing Activities

Commuting

Using the information in the chart on p.102 in your main textbook, write a series of statements about the location, distance from school, and convenience of the homes of each of the following people. Activity 3 on p.102 provides examples of the types of statements you could write.

1. カワムラさん：

_____

_____

_____

2. はやしさん：

_____

_____

_____

3. よこい先生：

_____

_____

_____

4. チンさん：

_____

_____

_____

5. おおの先生：

_____

_____

_____

6. Now tell about your own home:

_____

_____

_____

Cities and Neighborhoods

A. Fill in the blanks to create a meaningful sentence or phrase. Write in *X* if no additional word or particle is needed.

1. 大きい _____ うち

2. 小さい _____ アパート

3. しずか _____ 町

4. にぎやか _____ きんじょ

5. あたらしい _____ くるま

6. おもしろい _____ 本

7. きれい _____ 大学

8. わたしのうちはひろい _____ 。

9. みむらさんのアパートはせまい _____ 。

10. わたしの大学は有名 _____ 。

11. わたしのきんじょはしずか _____ 。

12. とうきょうのアパートはやすく _____ 。

13. ニューヨークはくるまがすくなく _____ 。

14. この本はよく _____ 。

15. この町はしずかでは _____ 。

16. わたしのアパートはきれいでは _____ 。

17. 先生のうちは大きいうち _____ 。

18. わたしのアパートはべんり _____ アパートです。

B. Write dialogues in which you ask Kawamura whether his home is near various places. After he answers, add a comment on whether the distance is convenient or inconvenient. Use the information on the following chart.

Places	Transportation	Time
station	on foot	six minutes
supermarket	on foot	fifteen minutes
movie theater	bus	thirty minutes
bus stop	on foot	one minute
bank	electric train	fifteen minutes
post office	bus	one hour

EXAMPLE: YOU: カワムラさんのうちはえきに近いですか。
KAWAMURA: ええ、あるいて6分です。
YOU: それはべんりですねえ。

1.   YOU: _____ 1

     KAWAMURA: _____ 2

        YOU: _____ 3

2.   YOU: _____ 1

     KAWAMURA: _____ 2

        YOU: _____ 3

3.   YOU: _____ 1

     KAWAMURA: _____ 2

        YOU: _____ 3

4.   YOU: _____ 1

     KAWAMURA: _____ 2

        YOU: _____ 3

5.   YOU: _____ 1

     KAWAMURA: _____ 2

        YOU: _____ 3

C. Imagine that a Japanese student is asking you for information about various places in the United States. Tell this student at least three things about each place, making an effort to use the adjectives you have learned in this chapter.

EXAMPLE: JAPANESE STUDENT: ニューヨークはどんなところですか。
              YOU: 大きい町です。おもしろいところですよ。でも (but) ちょっとやかましい
                    (noisy) です。

1. (イエローストーンパーク) _____

_____

2. (サンフランシスコ) _____

_____

3. ([イリノイの] ピオリア) _____

_____

4. (ニューオリンズ) _____

_____

Buildings and Places Around Town

A. Complete each sentence with either あります or います。

1. きょうしつに、先生が_____。

2. うちに、小さいいぬが_____。

3. めじろに、チンさんのアパートが_____。

4. この町に、大きいスーパーが_____。

5. としょかんに、本がたくさん_____。

B. A Japanese student wants to know where the following places are. Tell him or her which city or state they are located in.

EXAMPLE: JAPANESE STUDENT: イエローストーンパークはどこにありますか。
          YOU: ワイオミングにありますよ。

1. （ホワイトハウス）

   JAPANESE STUDENT: _____ 1

               YOU: _____ 2

2. （ディズニーワールド）

   JAPANESE STUDENT: _____ 1

               YOU: _____ 2

3. （エンパイアステートビル）

   JAPANESE STUDENT: _____ 1

               YOU: _____ 2

4. （グランドキャニオン）

   JAPANESE STUDENT: _____ 1

               YOU: _____ 2

C. Complete the following dialogues, using the information on the company message board pictured on p. 108 in your main textbook.

1. A: すみません。山田さんはいまどこにいますか。

   B: たかださんのオフィスに _____。

   A: 何時に、かえりますか。

   B: ごご三時ごろに、_____。

2. A: すみません。田中さんはいまどこにいますか。

   B: レストラン _____ います。

   A: 何時 _____ かえりますか。

   B: _____ 二時ごろに、かえります。

3. A: すみません。よしださんはいま _____ にいますか。

   B: ニューヨーク _____ います。

   A: いつ、かえりますか。

   B: あした、_____。

4. A: _____。さいとうさんは、_____ どこに _____ か。

   B: _____ にいます。

A: _____ にかえりますか。

B: ごご _____ ごろに、かえります。

5. A: _____。さわいさんは、いまどにに _____ か。

B: ひろしま _____。

A: いつ、_____。

B: らいしゅうの月よう日に _____。

D. Answer the questions about the following drawing. Choose your answers from among the options listed.
本 ／ かばん ／ えんぴつ ／ つくえ ／ まど ／ ねこ ／ とけい ／ こくばん ／ いす ／ 先生のつくえ ／ 先生 ／
田中さん ／ まど ／ しんぶん ／ かさ

1. つくえの上に何がありますか。 _____

2. つくえの下に何がありますか。 _____

3. かばんの中に何がありますか。 _____

4. かばんの右に何がありますか。 _____

5. つくえの左に何がありますか。 _____

6. 外に何がいますか。 _____

7. 田中さんの前にだれがいますか。 _____

8. 田中さんの後ろに何がありますか。 _____

9. つくえのそばに何がありますか。 _____

10. こくばんの前に何がありますか。 _____

11. こくばんとまどの間に何がありますか。 _____

E. Add the following items to the drawing to match the descriptive sentences below. Don't worry about creating great art. A rough sketch will be sufficient.

1. 先生のつくえの上に、ノートがあります。
2. いすの下に、大きいいぬがいます。
3. とけいの下に、大きいえ (picture) があります。
4. ねこのとなりに、小さいねずみ (mouse) がいます。
5. かばんの中に、セーターがあります。
6. 学生のつくえの上に、小さいコンピュータがあります。

F. Complete the following dialogues according to the guidelines given in parentheses.

1. (A is looking for the post office, which is a small, white [しろい] building across from a bank.)

   A: すみません。_____1 はありますか。

   B: ええ、_____2 にありますよ。

   A: どんなたてものですか。

   B: _____3 たてものですよ。

   A: どうもありがとうございました。

   B: どういたしまして。

2. (A is looking for a certain coffee shop, which is a pretty, blue [あおい] building near the university.)

   A: すみません。_____1 はありますか。

   B: ええ、_____2 にありますよ。

   A: どんなたてものですか。

   B: _____3 たてものですよ。

   A: どうもありがとうございました。

   B: _____4。

3. (A is looking for the police box, which is a small, black [くろい] building in front of the station.)

   A: すみません。_____1 はありますか。

   B: ええ、_____2 にありますよ。

   A: どんなたてものですか。

   B: _____3 たてものですよ。

   A: _____4。

   B: どういたしまして。

G. Complete the following dialogues according to the guidelines given in parentheses.

1. (A is looking for a good coffee shop. There is one called Kasaburanka near the university.)

   A: このきんじょに、いいきっさてんはありますか。

   B: ええ、_____1 よ。

   A: どこにありますか。

   B: 大学の_____2 にあります。

A: 名前は。

B: 「カサブランカ」です。

2. (A is looking for a large department store. There is one called Daitoku across from the subway station.)

A: このきんじょに、_____1 はありますか。

B: ええ、ありますよ。

A: どこにありますか。

B: _____2 のえきの _____3 にあります。

A: _____4 は。

B: 「だいとく」_____5

3. (A is looking for a cheap parking lot. There is one south of the hospital, but B doesn't know its name.)

A: このきんじょに、_____1 はありますか。

B: ええ、ありますよ。

A: _____2 にありますか。

B: びょういんの _____3 にあります。

A: _____4 は。

B: さあ、わかりません。

4. (A is looking for the new hotel. It's east of the restaurant, and it's called the Hotel Miyako.)

A: このきんじょに、_____1 はありますか。

B: ええ、ありますよ。

A: _____2 にありますか。

B: レストランの _____3 にあります。

A: _____4 は。

B: 「ホテルみやこ」です。

5. (A is looking for a quiet park. There is one called Chuuoo Kooen behind the library.)

A: このきんじょに、_____1 はありますか。

B: ええ、ありますよ。

A: _____2 にありますか。

B: _____3 の _____4 にあります。

A: 名前は。

B: 「ちゅうおうこうえん」です。

H. Write dialogues in which you ask a Japanese person for directions. Follow the guidelines given in parentheses.

1. (You'd like to know where the JR station is. It is next to a large department store.)

YOU: _____1

       JAPANESE: _____ 2

       _____

2. (You want to know what kind of building the post office is. It's a large building.)

       YOU: _____ 1

       JAPANESE: _____ 2

       _____

3. (You want to know what that big, white building is. It's a hotel.)

       YOU: _____ 1

       JAPANESE: _____ 2

4. (You'd like to find out where the big park is. It's in front of the university.)

       YOU: _____ 1

       JAPANESE: _____ 2

       _____

5. (You'd like to know what is above the station building. There's a department store.)

       YOU: _____ 1

       JAPANESE: _____ 2

       _____

6. (You'd like to know if there is a convenient parking lot nearby. It's behind a movie theater.)

       YOU: _____ 1

       JAPANESE: _____ 2

7. (You want to find out if there is a big hospital around here. You also want to know its name. It's between the park and the university, and it's called Meeji Byooin.)

       YOU: _____ 1

       JAPANESE: _____ 2

       YOU: _____ 3

       JAPANESE: _____ 4

I. Answer the following questions based on your actual situation.

1. あなたのかぞく (family) はいまどこにいますか。

       _____

2. ボーイフレンド／ガールフレンドがいますか。いまどこにいますか。

       _____

3. ルームメートがいますか。いまどこにいますか。

_____

4. あなたの日本語の先生はどこにいますか。(Guess if you don't know.)

_____

5. あなたのへや (or アパート or いえ) の右のへや (or アパート or いえ) にだれがいますか。左のへや (or アパート or いえ) は。じゃあ、前のへや (or アパート or いえ) は。

(右) _____

(左) _____

(前) _____

Counting

A. How many people do you need to play the following games? Answer in hiragana. Then see if you can write the answer in kanji.

	HIRAGANA	KANJI
EXAMPLE: やきゅう	じゅうはちにん	_____
1. バスケットボール	_____	_____
2. バレーボール	_____	_____
3. サッカー	_____	_____
4. マージャン	_____	_____
5. ポーカー	_____	_____
6. テニス	_____	_____
7. アメリカンフットボール	_____	_____
8. ラケットボール	_____	_____
9. ジョギング	_____	_____

B. Complete the following dialogues according to the guidelines given in parentheses.

1. (There are three men and two women on the basketball team.)

    A: 町田さんのバスケットボールのチームに学生は何人いますか。

    B: 五人です。

    A: みんなおとこの人ですか。

    B: いいえ、おとこの人が _____ とおんなの人が _____ います。

2. (There are three Japanese and one Chinese mah-jongg players.)

    A: みむらさんのマージャンのメンバーに学生は _____ いますか。

    B: _____ です。

    A: みんな日本人ですか。

    B: いいえ、日本人が _____ とちゅうごく人が _____ います。

3. (There are five teachers and 35 students in the orchestra.)

A: 山口さんのオーケストラに人が何人 _____ か。

B: _____ です。

A: みんな学生ですか。

B: いいえ、学生が _____ と先生が _____ います。

C. Answer the following questions about your own likes and dislikes.

1. にくが好きですか。 _____

2. やさいが好きですか。 _____

3. 日本のビールが好きですか。 _____

4. テレビが好きですか。 _____

5. ジョギングが好きですか。 _____

6. どんな人が好きですか。 _____

7. どんなくるまが好きですか。 _____

8. どんなレストランが好きですか。 _____

9. どんな本が好きですか。 _____

10. どんな町が好きですか。 _____

D. Brown polled her classmates and instructor on their likes and dislikes and wrote up the results on the following chart. Answer the questions using the information presented on the chart.

	たばこ	おさけ	さかな	やさい	コーヒー
ブラウン	きらい	きらい	好き	好き	好き
カーティス	きらい	好き	きらい	好き	きらい
カワムラ	きらい	好き	好き	きらい	好き
ギブソン	きらい	きらい	好き	好き	きらい
よこい	きらい	好き	きらい	好き	好き
はやし	好き	好き	きらい	好き	好き

1. たばこがきらいな人は何人いますか。_____
2. おさけがきらいな人は何人いますか。_____
3. さかなが好きな人は何人いますか。_____
4. やさいがきらいな人は何人いますか。_____
5. コーヒーが好きな人は何人いますか。_____

Now write two statements based on the information on the chart.

1. _____
2. _____

E. Make up a statement based on the information given.

EXAMPLE: books/in my room/50
わたしのへやに本が五十さつあります。

Remember?

Location に Noun は／が Quantity います (animate)／あります (inanimate)

or

Noun は／が Location に Quantity います (animate)／あります (inanimate)

---

1. students/in the library/2

_____

2. instructor/in front of the classroom/1

_____

3. a bank/in this town/4

_____

4. cafeteria/at the university/5

_____

5. a hospital/next to the post office/1

_____

F. Using your local telephone book, answer the following questions about the people and businesses in your community.

あなたの町に：

1. ぎんこうは何けんありますか。_____
2. ピザレストランは何けんありますか。_____
3. 日本レストランは何けんありますか。_____
4. 大きいスーパーは何けんありますか。_____

5. 田中さんは何人いますか。 _____

6. ブラウンさんは何人いますか。 _____

G. Form a study group of five people (or call up five of your classmates on the phone if you can't get together), and report on the following after asking the members of your group appropriate questions in Japanese.

EXAMPLE:　How many people like ice cream? How many people dislike it?
アイスクリームが好きな人は五人います。
アイスクリームがきらいな人はいません。

1. How many people like the current President (だいとうりょう) of the U.S.A.? How many dislike the President?

だいとうりょうが好きな人は _____。

だいとうりょうがきらいな人は _____。

2. How many people like your favorite musical group? How many people dislike them?

_____

_____

3. How many people like broccoli? How many dislike it?

_____

_____

4. How many people like New York as a place to live? How many dislike it?

_____

_____

Now make up four similar questions of your own, ask the members of your group, and write up the results.

H. Describe the following in at least three sentences. You may use either affirmative or negative statements, and you are encouraged to use adverbs such as とても and あまり, if you can.

1. your room _____

_____

2. your advisor _____

_____

3. your car or bicycle (If you don't have one, write about the one you would like to have.) _____

_____

4. one of your family members _____

_____

5. your girlfriend/boyfriend (actual or ideal) _____

_____

I. Answer the following questions, giving as many details as possible.

EXAMPLE:　どんな人が好きですか。
しんせつな人が好きです。まじめな人も好きです。

1. どんなくるまが好きですか。_____

2. どんな先生が好きですか。_____

3. どんな町が好きですか。_____

4. どんな大学が好きですか。_____

J. Answer the following questions about your home.

1. あなたのいえにへやはいくつありますか。_____

2. いすはいくつありますか。_____

3. テレビは何だいありますか。_____

4. 人は何人いますか。_____

5. 本は何さつありますか。(If you don't know, guess.) _____

6. ペットは何びきいますか。_____

K. The following is the seating chart for Professor Arai's classroom for the second term of the school year. Use it to figure out who the following five people are based on their descriptions of where they are. The top of the diagram corresponds to the front of the classroom.

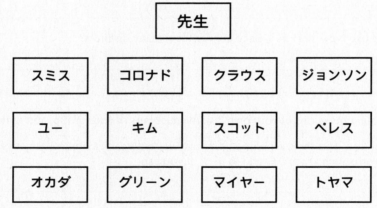

1. わたしはクラスの後ろにいます。わたしの右にはマイヤーさんがいます。

_____

2. わたしはユーさんとスコットさんの間にいます。

_____

3. わたしのとなりにはクラウスさんがいます。わたしの後ろはペレスさんです。

_____

4. わたしは先生のむかいにいます。わたしのとなりはスミスさんです。

_____

5. わたしはきょうしつの前にいます。わたしは学生じゃありません。

_____

L. John Kawamura is moving into his new room. He would like to have certain furniture and other things placed according to his directions. Please help him move in by drawing pictures of the various items in the appropriate places on the drawing. (おいてください means "Please place/put it.") Again, you don't have to produce great art.

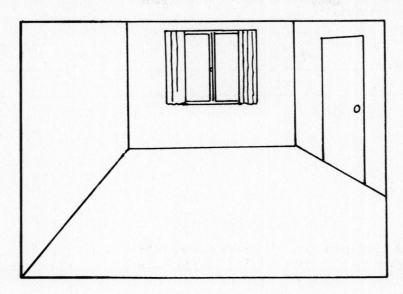

EXAMPLE:　このへやの右のコーナーにベッドをおいてください。

1.　ベッドの左に小さいテーブルをおいてください。ラジオはそのテーブルの上においてください。
2.　まどの前に大きいつくえをおいてください。つくえの上にスタンド (lamp) とでんわをおいてください。あ、コンピュータとキーボードもおねがいします。
3.　そのいすはつくえの前においてください。
4.　ドアのむかいのかべのところに、テレビと本だなをおいてください。あ、すみません。テレビと本だなの間にステレオをおいてください。

M. Now draw a diagram of your room. Describe the locations of at least six items. Remember the difference between <u>X</u> は <u>Y</u> にあります (The <u>X</u> is in location <u>Y</u>) and <u>Y</u> に <u>X</u> があります (In location <u>Y</u> there is an <u>X</u>.)

1. _____
2. _____
3. _____
4. _____
5. _____
6. _____

N. Write as much as you can about each of the items below, following the example:

EXAMPLE:　your favorite drink
　　　　　わたしの好きなのみものはコーヒーです。あついのみものが大好きです。

1. your favorite food _____
_____

2. your favorite city in the U.S. _____
_____

3. your least favorite subject at college _____

_____

4. your least favorite instructor _____

_____

5. your favorite car _____

_____

CHAPTER **3**

日常生活

Listening Comprehension Activities

Schedules

A. Listen to the passage about Satoo's typical week. Then mark each of the following statements either true(T) or false(F).

1. _____ Satoo is from Los Angeles.

2. _____ Satoo is not a student.

3. _____ During the week, Satoo is very busy at work.

4. _____ On Saturdays, Satoo does a variety of things.

5. _____ Satoo goes out on Sunday nights.

B. Listen to the conversation between Antonio Coronado and Midori Momoi. Then complete the English summary by filling in the blanks. Some blanks may contain more than one word.

Midori has _____ this afternoon, and she is busy tomorrrow because she has to

_____ . Saturday, April _____, is her birthday. She will

_____ Saturday night, which will be at _____ o'clock. Antonio

_____ her invitation.

C. Professor Arai's students have planned a party for her. Listen to the conversation in which they tell her about it. Then complete the sentences below by circling the correct answer.

USEFUL VOCABULARY

どうして (ですか)	*why*
それで	*then*
…から	*because . . .*

1. Professor Arai is usually busy in the (a. morning b. afternoon c. evening) every day.

2. Today is (a. August b. September c. October) 2nd.

3. Tomorrow is (a. Wednesday b. Thursday c. Friday).

4. September 4th is (a. Wednesday b. Thursday c. Friday).

5. Professor Arai's birthday is (a. today b. tomorrow c. the day after tomorrrow).

Daily Activities

A. Listen as Hans Kraus, Midori Momoi, and Ryan Scott describe their morning activities. Then complete each sentence by filling in the initial of the person it best describes. (K: Kraus   M: Midori   S: Scott)

USEFUL VOCABULARY

すぐ	*right away*
それで	*so, therefore*
はやく	*early* (adv.)
(…の) あと	*after . . .*

1. _____ jogs.

2. _____ doesn't eat breakfast.

3. _____ drinks orange juice.

4. _____ gets up at 7:00.

5. _____ goes to school by bus.

6. _____ walks to school.

7. _____ has morning classes only twice a week.

8. _____ drives to school.

9. _____ studies before leaving home.

10. _____ takes 10 minutes to go to school.

11. _____ leaves home at 9:00.

12. _____ sometimes eats lunch at home.

B. Professor Arai has assigned Antonio Coronado and Peggy Yu to be conversation partners. Listen to their conversation, and then complete each sentence by writing in the initial of the person it refers to. (C: Coronado   S: Smith   Y: Yu   N: none of the three)

EXAMPLE: <u>C and S</u> eat at home during the week.

1. _____ likes cooking.

2. _____ eats out on weekends.

3. _____ practices Japanese a lot.

4. _____ often eats at the University cafeteria.

5. _____ prefers washing dishes to cooking.

6. _____ prefers staying at home on weekends.

7. _____ is lucky to live with a good cook.

8. _____ gives parties at home on weekends.

C. Professor Arai and Ryan Scott run into each other one afternoon on campus. Listen to their conversation, and then answer the following questions in English.

USEFUL VOCABULARY

じつは	*to tell the truth*
おそく	*late* (adv.)
しけん	*exam*

1. Why did Scott miss class this morning? _____

_____

2. What did he do last night? _____

_____

3. What is he going to do this evening? _____

_____

4. What is he going to do tomorrow? _____

_____

5. When is the exam? _____

_____

D. Midori Momoi has received a letter from her friend, Noriko, who is studying in Tokyo. Actually, Noriko wrote to her parents on the same day. You will hear both letters read out loud. After listening to them, identify the following statements, by writing *P* next to those found in the letter written to her parents, *M* next to those found in the letter written to Momoi and *P/M* next to those found in both letters.

USEFUL VOCABULARY

が	*but*
せいかつ	*life, way of life*
ねむい	*sleepy*
かりる	*to borrow*
りょこう	*a trip*

Noriko:

1. _____ is very busy.

2. _____ gets up early every morning.

3. _____ studies in the library all the time.

4. _____ doesn't go out at all.

5. _____ works at night.

6. _____ misses her morning classes often.

7. _____ has no time to watch TV.

8. _____ will have a difficult exam next week.

9. _____ will borrow notes from a friend to prepare for the exam.

10. _____ will have to study hard all this week.

E. There was a robbery last night at the company where Murayama works. Listen as the policeman questions Murayama. Then mark the following statements either true(T) or false(F).

USEFUL VOCABULARY

(…の) あいだ	*between*
だれも (+ *negative*)	*no one*
へん (な)	*strange*
となり (の)	*neighboring*

1. _____ Yesterday, at 7 P.M., both Murayama and Toda were still at work.

2. _____ Murayama left work later than Toda.

3. _____ Murayama took a train to Tokyo Station.

4. _____ Murayama didn't go home directly.

5. _____ Murayama didn't eat dinner yesterday.

6. _____ Murayama didn't see anyone after she left work.

7. _____ Toda was in Shinjuku around 10 P.M.

8. _____ Toda and Murayama live far away from each other.

9. _____ Toda took a train to go home from Shinjuku.

10. _____ Toda took the same train as Murayama.

F. Professor Arai is asking her students about their athletic activities. Listen to the conversation, and find out what kind of sports each person participates in and how often.

USEFUL VOCABULARY

たいてい	usually
(…の)とき	when . . .

		sports	*how often*
1.	Professor Arai:	_____	_____
2.	Smith:	_____	_____
3.	Kraus:	_____	_____
4.	Yu:	_____	_____

G. Listen as Honda continues his interview of Himiko. Then complete the following sentences by circling the correct answer.

USEFUL VOCABULARY

…だけ	only
びよういん	beauty shop

1. _____ Himiko usually gets up at around (a. 10   b. 11   c. 12) o'clock.

2. _____ Himiko brushes her teeth (a. more often than   b. as often as   c. less often than) she takes a bath every day.

3. _____ Honda takes a bath three times a (a. day   b. week   c. month).

4. _____ Himiko goes to the beauty shop (a. every day   b. before work   c. both a and b).

5. _____ Himiko practices dancing (a. more often than   b. as often as   c. less often than) she eats every day.

6. _____ Honda eats (a. more often than   b. as often as   c. less often than) Himiko.

7. _____ Himiko drinks a (a. glass   b. bottle   c. case) of champagne every day.

8. _____ Honda (a. sometimes   b. seldom   c. never) drinks champagne.

9. _____ Honda watches movies (a. more often than   b. as often as   c. less often than) Himiko.

Weekdays and Weekends

A. The last sentence of each of the following five dialogues is incomplete. You will hear each dialogue read twice. Then choose the best completion from the righthand column, and write its letter in the appropriate blank in the lefthand column. You will use each option only once.

1. _____
2. _____
3. _____
4. _____
5. _____

a. じてんしゃにのります。
b. うちにいます。
c. ひまです。
d. テニスをします。
e. ねぼうします。

B. Listen as Satoo and Momoi talk about their weekend activities. Find out which one of the two (S: Satoo M: Momoi) does the following.

USEFUL VOCABULARY

めったに (+ negative)   *seldom, rarely*

1. _____ goes to the movies frequently.

2. _____ seldom goes to the movies.

3. _____ does some housework on weekends.

4. _____ is active on Saturday afternoons.

5. _____ relaxes on Sundays.

6. _____ studies on Sunday nights.

7. _____ often goes drinking on Saturday nights.

C. It is Sunday afternoon, and Midori Momoi and Lois Johnson, who have finished the weekend's homework, are sitting around, wondering how to pass the time. Listen to their conversation, and then mark each of the following statements either true (T) or false (F).

USEFUL VOCABULARY

こむ	*to get crowded*
かんがえ	*idea*
もう (+ *negative*)	*not anymore, no longer*
もういちど	*once more*
…まえに	*before...*
さいこう	*the greatest*
かたづける	*to tidy up*

1. _____ Midori Momoi and Lois Johnson decide not to go to the movies because they don't have any money.

2. _____ They decide to invite Cody Smith and Antonio Coronado over for dinner because Cody and Antonio are interesting people.

3. _____ There's no cola left because Midori forgot to buy some at the supermarket.

4. _____ Midori really likes Lois's spaghetti sauce.

5. _____ Cody and Antonio are late for dinner.

6. _____ Midori tells Lois not to come into the kitchen.

7. _____ The last time Cody and Antonio were there they washed the dishes.

8. _____ Lois decides to tidy up the room.

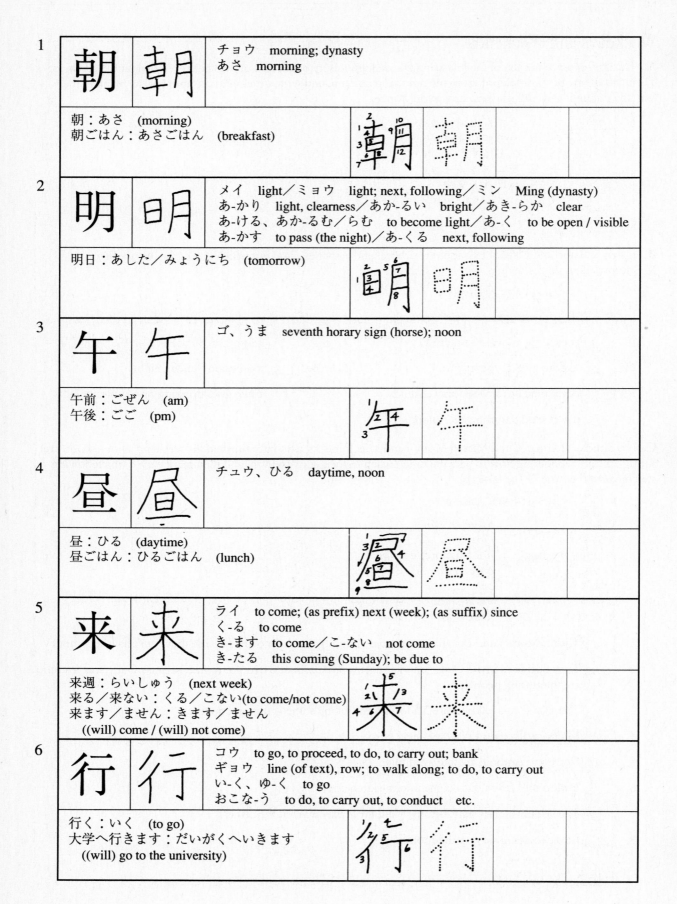

1	朝　朝	チョウ　morning; dynasty あさ　morning
	朝：あさ　(morning) 朝ごはん：あさごはん　(breakfast)	
2	明　明	メイ　light／ミョウ　light; next, following／ミン　Ming (dynasty) あ-かり　light, clearness／あか-るい　bright／あき-らか　clear あ-ける、あか-るむ／らむ　to become light／あ-く　to be open / visible あ-かす　to pass (the night)／あ-くる　next, following
	明日：あした／みょうにち　(tomorrow)	
3	午　午	ゴ、うま　seventh horary sign (horse); noon
	午前：ごぜん　(am) 午後：ごご　(pm)	
4	昼　昼	チュウ、ひる　daytime, noon
	昼：ひる　(daytime) 昼ごはん：ひるごはん　(lunch)	
5	来　来	ライ　to come; (as prefix) next (week); (as suffix) since く-る　to come き-ます　to come／こ-ない　not come き-たる　this coming (Sunday); be due to
	来週：らいしゅう　(next week) 来る／来ない：くる／こない(to come/not come) 来ます／ません：きます／ません 　((will) come / (will) not come)	
6	行　行	コウ　to go, to proceed, to do, to carry out; bank ギョウ　line (of text), row; to walk along; to do, to carry out い-く、ゆ-く　to go おこな-う　to do, to carry out, to conduct　etc.
	行く：いく　(to go) 大学へ行きます：だいがくへいきます 　((will) go to the university)	

7	聞	聞	ブン、モン、き-く　to hear, to listen to, to heed, to ask き-こえる　to be heard / audible き-こえ　reputation, publicity			
	聞く：きく　(to listen / ask) ラジオを聞きます：らじおをききます 　((will) listen to the radio) しん聞：しんぶん　(newspaper)			聞	聞	
8	食	食	ショク、ショッ、ジキ　food, eating た-べる　to eat く-う／らう　to eat, to drink, to receive (a blow) く-える　can eat			
	食べる：たべる　(to eat) 朝ごはんを食べます：あさごはんをたべます 　((will) eat breakfast)			食	食	
9	出	出	シュツ、シュッ-、すい、で-る　to go/come out, to appear, to emerge で　one's turn; origin だ-す　to put/take out, to send; (as verb suffix) begin to...			
	出かける：でかける　(to go out) 出かけます：でかけます　((will) go out) 出る：でる　(to leave (home)) 出ます：でます　((will) leave (home))			出	出	
10	飲	飲	イン、の-む　to drink			
	飲む：のむ　(to drink) コーヒーを飲みました：こーひーをのみました 　((I) drank coffee)			飲	飲	
11	入	入	ニュウ、ジュ、はい-る、い-る　to go/come in, to enter い-れる　to put/let in			
	入る：はいる　(to go in) 入ります：はいります　((will) go in) 入れる：いれる　(to put in) 入れます：いれます　((will) put in)			入	入	
12	休	休	キュウ、やす-む　to rest, to take time off やす-める　to rest, to set at ease やす-まる　to be rested, to feel at ease やす-み　rest, break, vacation; absence			
	休む：やすむ　(to rest) 休みましょう：やすみましょう 　(Let's take a rest) 休みの日：やすみのひ　(holiday)			休	休	

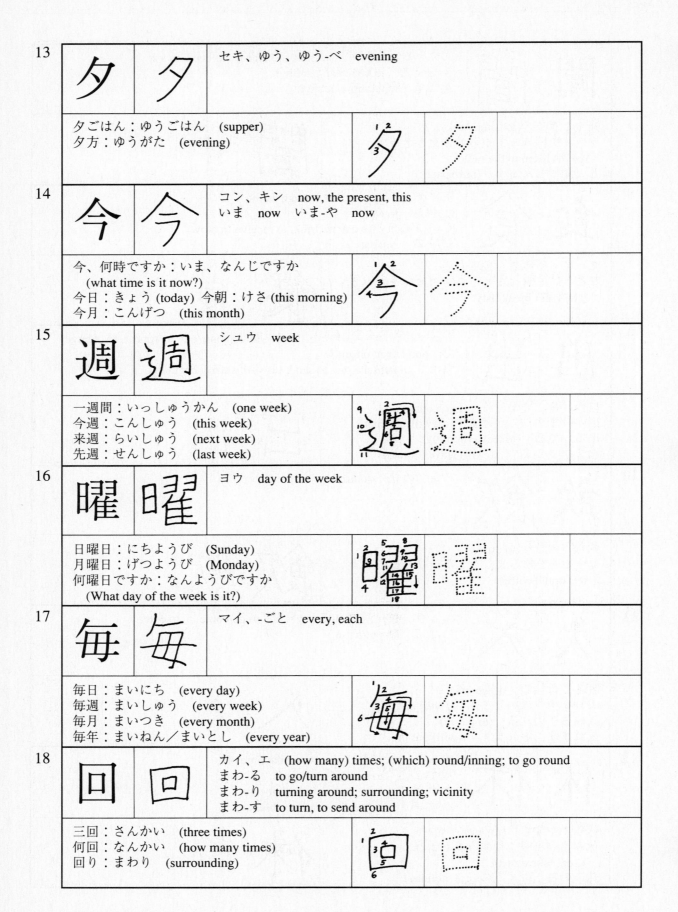

13	夕　夕	セキ、ゆう、ゆう-べ　evening
	夕ごはん：ゆうごはん　(supper) 夕方：ゆうがた　(evening)	

14	今　今	コン、キン　now, the present, this いま　now　いま-や　now
	今、何時ですか：いま、なんじですか 　(what time is it now?) 今日：きょう (today)　今朝：けさ (this morning) 今月：こんげつ　(this month)	

15	週　週	シュウ　week
	一週間：いっしゅうかん　(one week) 今週：こんしゅう　(this week) 来週：らいしゅう　(next week) 先週：せんしゅう　(last week)	

16	曜　曜	ヨウ　day of the week
	日曜日：にちようび　(Sunday) 月曜日：げつようび　(Monday) 何曜日ですか：なんようびですか 　(What day of the week is it?)	

17	毎　毎	マイ、-ごと　every, each
	毎日：まいにち　(every day) 毎週：まいしゅう　(every week) 毎月：まいつき　(every month) 毎年：まいねん／まいとし　(every year)	

18	回　回	カイ、エ　(how many) times; (which) round/inning; to go round まわ-る　to go/turn around まわ-り　turning around; surrounding; vicinity まわ-す　to turn, to send around
	三回：さんかい　(three times) 何回：なんかい　(how many times) 回り：まわり　(surrounding)	

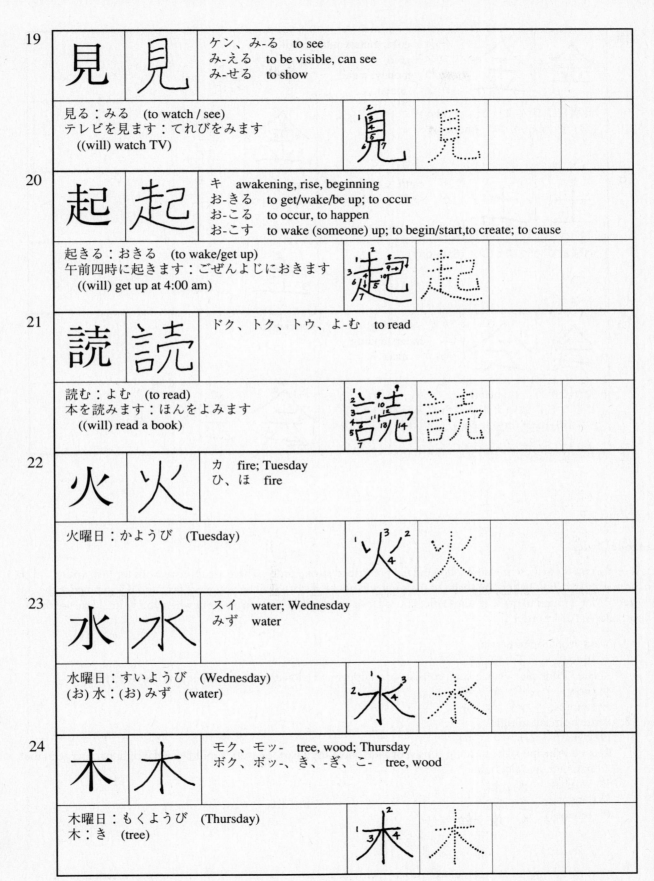

19 見 見

ケン、み-る　to see
み-える　to be visible, can see
み-せる　to show

見る：みる　(to watch / see)
テレビを見ます：てれびをみます
　((will) watch TV)

20 起 起

キ　awakening, rise, beginning
お-きる　to get/wake/be up; to occur
お-こる　to occur, to happen
お-こす　to wake (someone) up; to begin/start, to create; to cause

起きる：おきる　(to wake/get up)
午前四時に起きます：ごぜんよじにおきます
　((will) get up at 4:00 am)

21 読 読

ドク、トク、トウ、よ-む　to read

読む：よむ　(to read)
本を読みます：ほんをよみます
　((will) read a book)

22 火 火

カ　fire; Tuesday
ひ、ほ　fire

火曜日：かようび　(Tuesday)

23 水 水

スイ　water; Wednesday
みず　water

水曜日：すいようび　(Wednesday)
(お) 水：(お) みず　(water)

24 木 木

モク、モッ-　tree, wood; Thursday
ボク、ボッ-、き、-ぎ、こ-　tree, wood

木曜日：もくようび　(Thursday)
木：き　(tree)

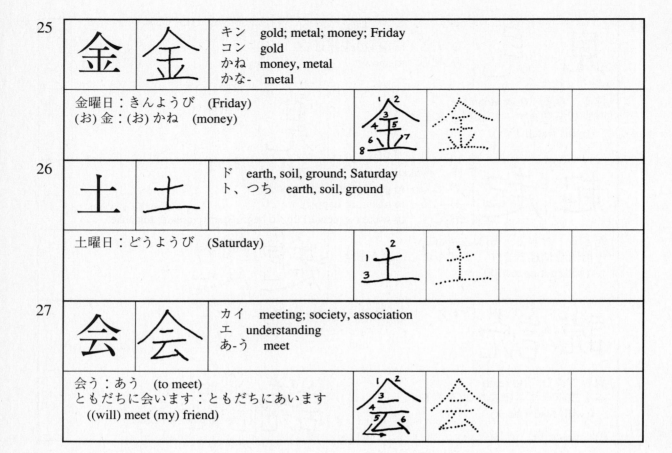

25	金 金	キン gold; metal; money; Friday コン gold かね money, metal かな- metal
	金曜日：きんようび (Friday) (お) 金：(お) かね (money)	
26	土 土	ド earth, soil, ground; Saturday ト、つち earth, soil, ground
	土曜日：どようび (Saturday)	
27	会 会	カイ meeting; society, association エ understanding あ-う meet
	会う：あう (to meet) ともだちに会います：ともだちにあいます ((will) meet (my) friend)	

KANJI NOTE

Stroke Order

It is important that you write kanji following the prescribed stroke order. There are three reasons for this: your handwriting will look better, the shape of the kanji will not be distorted when you write fast, and if you practice the correct order enough to make it automatic, you will not accidentally leave strokes out when you write. Here are the basic rules of stroke order.

1. Write from top to bottom.
   三 (three)   一 二 三
   Related Principle: when a kanji consists of an upper and a lower part, the upper part is written first.
   今 (now)   ハ 今 今
   分 (minute)   ハ 今 分
2. Write from left to right.
   川 (river)   丿 川 川
   Related Principle: when a kanji consist of a left and a right part, or a left, a middle, and a right part, write in the order of left, middle, right.
   林 (woods)   木 林
   語 (language)   言 語
   働 (to work)   イ 働 働

3. When a vertical and a horizontal line cross, the vertical line is written before the horizontal line.
十 (ten)　　一　十
七 (seven)　一　七
大 (large)　一　ナ　大
Exceptions:
(1) 田 and related kanji
田 (rice paddy)　冂　m　田
町 (town)　　　　田　町　町
男 (man)　　　　　　　　男
(2) 王 and related kanji
王 (king)　　一　丁　王
生 (life)　　ケ　牛　生

4. When a kanji consists of a left, a middle, and a right part and the left and right parts consist of one or two strokes each, the middle part is written first.
小 (small)　　亅　小　小
Exception:
火 (fire)　　　丶　ソ　火

5. When a kanji has an enclosure, it is written first.
日 (day)　　　丨　冂　月　日
国 (country)　丿　冂　国　国

6. When two diagonal lines cross, the line from upper right to lower left is written first.
文 (sentence)　亠　亠　文
人 (person)　　丿　人

7. Lines that cross an entire kanji or part of it from top to bottom are written last.
中 (middle)　口　中
書 (to write)　亖　聿　書

8. Lines that cross an entire kanji from left to right are written last.
子 (child)　　了　子
女 (woman)　く　女　女
Exception:
世 (generation)　一　廿　世

9. In kanji including the radical *shinnyuu*, that radical is written last.
道 (street)　首　首　道
Exceptions:
起 (to get up)　走　起
勉 (to study)　免　勉

10. In kanji including the radical *tare*, that radical is written first.
店 (shop)　　广　店
庭 (garden)　广　庭

KANJI EXERCISES (3)

1. Match each kanji or compound with its closest English equivalent.

1. 曜 _____ 2. 読 _____ 3. 飲 _____

4. 食 _____ 5. 木 _____ 6. 見 _____

7. 聞 _____ 8. 会 _____ 9. 行 _____

10. 休 _____ 11. 出 _____ 12. 来 _____

13. 昼 _____ 14. 朝 _____ 15. 明日 _____

16. 今 _____ 17. 夕方 _____ 18. 週 _____

19. 午後 _____ 20. 土 _____ 21. 毎 _____

22. 入 _____ 23. 火 _____ 24. 起 _____

25. 三回 _____ 26. 金 _____ 27. 水 _____

(a) morning   (b) evening   (c) tomorrow   (d) now   (e) afternoon   (f) week   (g) daytime
(h) to come   (i) fire   (j) to meet   (k) to go   (l) to enter   (m) to listen   (n) to watch   (o) to eat
(p) to get up   (q) tree   (r) to read   (s) water   (t) three times   (u) day of a week   (v) every
(w) to rest   (x) gold/money   (y) soil   (z) to drink   (aa) to go/come out

2. Write the hurigana for each kanji or compound.

1. 毎朝 _____ 2. 夕方 _____ 3. 午前 _____

4. 読む _____ 5. 休む _____ 6. 飲む _____

7. 出かける _____ 8. 見る _____ 9. 入る _____

10. 昼 _____ 11. 行く _____ 12. 聞く _____

13. 会う _____ 14. 食べる _____ 15. 起きる _____

16. 来週 _____ 17. 今 _____ 18. 時々 _____

19. 午後 _____ 20. 二、三回 _____ 21. 金曜日 _____

22. 明日 _____ 23. 今日 _____ 24. 毎日 _____

25. 来ます _____ 26. 来る _____ 27. 来ない _____

28. 今年 _____ 29. 今週 _____ 30. 今月 _____

31. 一週間 _____ 32. 何回 _____ 33. 土曜日 _____

34. 木曜日 _____ 35. 水曜日 _____ 36. 火曜日 _____

3. Write the appropriate kanji for the hiragana under the lines.

1. _____<u>1</u> の _____<u>2</u> はひまです。
   あした   ごご

2. _____<u>1</u> の _____<u>2</u> は _____<u>3</u> ですか。
   らいしゅう   げつようび   なんにち

3. _____<u>1</u> _____<u>2</u> _____<u>3</u> きます。
   まいにち   ごじはん   お

4. _____1 に _____2 ごはんを _____3 べました。
   ろくじ あさ た

5. _____1 は、しんぶんを _____2 みませんでした。
   きょう よ

6. _____1 きっさてんでコーヒーを _____2 みます。
   ときどき の

7. _____1 に _____2 おふろに _____3 りますか。
   いっしゅうかん なんかい はい

8. _____1 ごはんを _____2 べましょう。
   ひる た

9. _____1 みの _____2 は _____3 をしますか。
   やす ひ なに

10. _____1、ともだちがうちへ _____2 ました。
   ゆうがた き

11. _____1 _____2 ですか。
   いま なんじ

12. おんがくを _____ きましょう。
   き

13. バスで _____1 へ _____2 きます。
   だいがく い

14. きのう、えいがを _____ ました。
   み

15. あには、カワムラさんと _____ かけました。
   で

16. わたしはフランス _____1 を _____2 します。
   ご はな

17. _____1 ともだちに _____2 います。
   あした あ

4. Write the kanji for the days of the week in order, starting with Sunday.

1. _____

2. _____

3. _____

4. _____

5. _____

6. _____

7. _____

Writing Activities

Schedules

A. Answer the following questions, based on this year's calendar.

1. クリスマスは何月何日ですか。

   _____

2. バレンタインデーは何月何日ですか。

   _____

3. エープリルフールは何月何日ですか。

   _____

4. 五月五日は何曜日ですか。

   _____

5. 九月八日は何曜日ですか。

   _____

6. 七月八日は何曜日ですか。

   _____

7. 八月二十四日は何曜日ですか。

   _____

8. 十月三十一日は何曜日ですか。

   _____

9. 十月三日は何曜日ですか。

   _____

10. 六月九日は何曜日ですか。

    _____

11. 来週の水曜日は何日ですか。

    _____

12. 今週の土曜日は何日ですか。

    _____

13. 来月の十三日は何曜日ですか。

    _____

14. 今月の二十九日は何曜日ですか。

    _____

15. 先週の木曜日は何日でしたか。（でした：it was, the past tense form of です.)

    _____

16. 先週の日曜日は何日でしたか。

_____

17. たんじょう日は何月何日ですか。

_____

18. 何年生まれですか。

_____

B. Today is Friday. Kawamura and three of his classmates have decided to go on a picnic, and they need to find a day when all of them are free. Fill in the schedule according to each person's description of his or her activities. Then decide what the best day for the picnic would be.

	this Saturday	this Sunday	next Saturday	next Sunday
Kawamura				
Brown				
Hayashi				
Machida				

カワムラ：わたしは明日はひまですが、あさってはクラブのミーティングがあります。来週は土曜日も日曜日もひまです。

ブラウン：今週も来週も土曜日はいいですけど、日曜日はきょうかいへ行きます。

はやし：明日はクラスがあります。午後三時ごろからはひまです。あさってもひまですよ。来週の土曜日はクラスがありませんけれども、日曜日はデートをしますから、ちょっと…。

町田：ごめんなさい。今週はとうきょうにいません。来週の金曜日のよるかえります。でも、日曜日にはまた出かけます。

The best day for the picnic is: _____.

C. Using this year's calendar, make up short dialogues about the dates and the days of the week of the following holidays. For Japanese holidays, you may refer to Chapter 3 of your main text.

EXAMPLE: (U.S.)(どくりつきねん日)(Independence Day)

Q: どくりつきねん日は何月何日ですか。今年のどくりつきねん日は何曜日です／でしたか。
A: 七月四日です。今年はX曜日でした。

1. マーティンルーサーキングデー (U.S.)

Q: _____ 1

A: _____ 2

2. あなたのたんじょう日 (Not really a holiday, but...)

Q: _____ 1

A: _____ 2

3. サンクスギビングデー (U.S.)
Q:サンクスギビングデーは何曜日ですか。今年のサンクスギビングデーは何月何日です／でしたか。

A: _____

4. こどもの日 (日本)

Q: _____ 1

A: _____ 2

5. けいろうの日 (日本)

Q: _____ 1

A: _____ 2

6. ぶんかの日 (日本)

Q: _____ 1

A: _____ 2

D. How would you ask questions in the following situations? Make up questions using such time expressions as 何年、何月、何日 etc.

You'd like to know:

1. when Linda's birthday is. _____

2. in what year she was born. _____

3. in which month she is returning to the U.S. _____

4. on which days of the week she has classes. _____

5. which day she has free time. _____

E. Looking at John's schedule for this month, ask when the following events took place / are going to take place. Then answer the questions about his schedule.

日	月	火	水	木	金	土
	1 しけん	2	3	4 バイト	5 プール	6 デート
7 バイト	8 たんじょう日	9	10 はいしゃ	11	12	13
14	15	16	17	18 バイト	19 プール	20 パーティー
21	22	23	24 しけん	25	26	27
28	29	30	31 コンサート			

USEFUL VOCABULARY

しけん　　　　*exam, test*
はいしゃ　　　*dentist*

バイト is short for アルバイト and is a slang term used by college students.

EXAMPLE: (exam)

YOU: しけんは何日の何曜日ですか。
JOHN: 一日の月曜日でした。それから、二十四日の水曜日にもあります。

1. (work)

YOU: _____ 1

JOHN: _____ 2

2. (swimming)

YOU: _____ 1

JOHN: _____ 2

3. (dentist's appointment)

YOU: _____ 1

JOHN: _____ 2

4. (date)

YOU: _____ 1

JOHN: _____ 2

5. (day off)

YOU: _____ 1

JOHN: _____ 2

6. (concert)

YOU: _____ 1

JOHN: _____ 2

Daily Activities

A. Look at Maria Nakajima's schedule and answer the following questions.

MARIA NAKAJIMA'S SCHEDULE

6:00 A.M.	get up
6:20	jogging
7:00	read the newspaper
8:00	drink juice
8:10	study English
9:30	leave for English class
12:00 P.M.	eat lunch
1:00	leave for work
8:00	go back home

9:00	eat dinner
10:00	watch TV
12:00	go to bed

1. なかじまさんは、毎日何時に起きますか。

_____

2. なかじまさんは、毎日朝ごはんを食べますか。

_____

3. 毎日六時二十分に何をしますか。

_____

4. 毎日七時に何をしますか。

_____

5. 毎日ジュースを飲みますか。

_____

6. 何時に出かけますか。

_____

7. 毎日何をべんきょうしますか。

_____

8. 午後一時から午後八時まで何をしますか。

_____

9. 十時から十二時まで何をしますか。

_____

10. 毎日何時にねますか。

_____

11. 毎日何時間べんきょうしますか。

_____

12. 毎日何時間ねますか。

_____

B. Answer the questions, based on the Maria Nakajima's schedule as shown in Exercise A.

1. なかじまさんは、何時にしんぶんを読みますか。

_____

2. それから、何をしますか。

_____

3. その後、何をしますか。

_____

4. なかじまさんは、何時に昼ごはんを食べますか。

   _____

5. その後、何をしますか。

   _____

6. なかじまさんは、何時にいえへかえりますか。

   _____

7. それから、何をしますか。

   _____

8. その後、何をしますか。

   _____

C. To which classes do the following verbs belong? Write the numbers in the blanks.

1. ___ 食べる
2. ___ 見る
3. ___ 読む
4. ___ 入る
5. ___ でんわする
6. ___ 来る
7. ___ 行く

8. ___ シャワーをあびる
9. ___ うちを出る
10. ___ 起きる
11. ___ ねる
12. ___ かえる
13. ___ 出かける
14. ___ ある

15. ___ いる
16. ___ あそぶ
17. ___ かく
18. ___ およぐ
19. ___ まつ
20. ___ 会う
21. ___ 話す

D. Here is a schedule of what Peggy Yu did yesterday. Use the information in the schedule to answer the questions.

PEGGY YU'S SCHEDULE

7:00 A.M.	got up
7:10	exercised
7:45	took a shower
8:30	ate breakfast
9:00	left home
10:00	went to her political science class
12:00 P.M.	went to her literature class
1:30	ate a banana
1:45	went to her friend's apartment
2:00	cooked spaghetti with her friend
2:30	ate spaghetti
5:00	returned home
5:15	phoned her friend
7:00	watched TV
9:00	listened to music
10:30	took a bath
11:00	went to bed

1. ユーさんは、きのう何時に起きましたか。

2. きのうの朝、何分うんどうしましたか。

3. きのう、シャワーをあびましたか。

4. おふろに入りましたか。

5. 昼ごはんを食べましたか。何を食べましたか。

6. ともだちに会いましたか。

7. 何のクラスに行きましたか。

8. 何をりょうりしましたか。

9. 何時にいえへかえりましたか。

10. ともだちにでんわしましたか。

11. 何時間ともだちと話しましたか。

12. えいがを見ましたか。

13. 何時間テレビを見ましたか。

14. しんぶんを読みましたか。

15. 何時にねましたか。

E. Read each of the questions in the lefthand column and choose *the best* answer from the righthand column. Some of the possible answers in the righthand column will not be used.

1. _____ 何を飲みましたか。
2. _____ うんどうしましたか。
3. _____ だれにでんわしましたか。
4. _____ どこへ行きましたか。
5. _____ テレビを見ましたか。
6. _____ 朝、ねぼうしましたか。
7. _____ シャワーをあびましたか。
8. _____ 本を読みましたか。

a. 八時に行きました。
b. ともだちにでんわしました。
c. いいえ、見ませんでした。
d. いいえ、コーヒーを飲みました。
e. はい、本を読みました。
f. おいしいおちゃを飲みました。
g. はい、うんどうしました。
h. はい、でんわしました。
i. いいえ、ねぼうしませんでした。
j. としょかんへ行きました。
k. はい、シャワーをあびました。

F. How often do you do the following activities? Read through the list of activities in the lefthand column and write in the letter of the time phrase which best describes how often you do each activity. You may use a time phrase more than once if it describes your actual situation.

EXAMPLE:　__f__ 大学へ行きます。

1. _____ 朝ごはんを食べます。
2. _____ シャワーをあびます。
3. _____ かおをあらいます。
4. _____ デートをします。
5. _____ かいものをします。
6. _____ そうじをします。
7. _____ ひげをそります。
8. _____ おさけを飲みます。
9. _____ りょうりをします。
10. _____ えいがを見ます。
11. _____ くるまをうんてんします。
12. _____ せんたくをします。
13. _____ さんぽします。
14. _____ はをみがきます。

a. 一日に一回
b. 一日に二回
c. 一日に三回
d. 一週間に一回
e. 一か月に一回
f. 毎日
g. 毎週
h. 毎月
i. いつも
j. よく
k. 時々
l. たまに
m. あまりしない
n. ぜんぜんしない

G. Answer the following questions based on your actual situation.

1. あなたは毎日何時に起きますか。_____
2. 何時に朝ごはんを食べますか。_____
3. 何時に大学へ行きますか。_____
4. 日曜日は何時に起きますか。_____
5. 土曜日は何時にねますか。_____
6. たいてい (usually) よる何時からべんきょうしますか。_____

H. On a separate sheet of paper jot down four or five things you plan to do tomorrow afternoon. Then write your plans in connected narrative form in the space below, remembering to use conjunctions such as それから、そして、 and その後 to make your paragraph flow smoothly.

_____

_____

_____

_____

_____

I. Interview three classmates (in Japanese) and find out if each of them did the following activities yesterday. If the answer is yes, ask what time s/he did it and record the time in the chart. If the answer is no, leave the box blank.

	Name	took shower	phoned friend	listened to music	studied	went to library
1						
2						
3						

J. On a separate piece of paper jot down four or five things you did yesterday afternoon. Then write a connected account in narrative form in the space below, remembering to use conjunctions such as それから、そして、 and その後 to make your paragraph flow smoothly.

_____

_____

_____

_____

_____

K. Interview a classmate in Japanese and find out how often he or she does the following things. State the answer in terms of number of times per day, week, month or year. Then give your opinion of the frequency of the action, using words such as いつも、よく、たまに、ぜんぜん、and others.

> EXAMPLE: _Your conversation_:
> YOU: スミスさんは一日何回ぐらいはをみがきますか。
> SMITH: 一日三回ぐらいみがきます。
> _Your report_: スミスさんは一日三回ぐらいはをみがきます。
> よくはをみがきます。

The name of the person you are reporting on: _____

1. (taking bath) _____

2. (changing clothes) _____

3. (driving a car) _____

4. (doing laundry) _____

5. (cooking) _____

6. (cleaning room) _____

7. (oversleeping) _____

8. (dating) _____

Weekends and Holidays

A. Complete each sentence with a verb. Be sure that the verb you choose makes sense in terms of meaning and in terms of the time words used.

1. きのう、としょかんで本を _____。

2. 明日、かいものを _____。

3. 先週、ともだちにでんわを _____。

4. 来週、田中さんとテニスを _____。

5. 来月、クラスが _____ (to start)。

6. 先月、クラスが _____ (to end)。

7. きょ年、日本へ _____。

8. 来年、スペイン語をべんきょう _____。

9. おととい、ぜんぜんテレビを _____。

10. 今週、あまりコーヒーを _____。

11. 毎朝、シャワーを _____。

12. 毎週、デートを _____。

13. 毎日、おんがくを _____。

14. 時々、てがみを _____。

B. You have learned a number of particles up to this point. Test yourself to see how well you have mastered the new ones and remember the old ones by filling in the blanks in the sentences below. Use *X* if no particle is needed.

1. わたし _____ 日本人です。

2. レストラン _____1 ハンバーガー _____2 食べ ましょう。

3. 毎日 _____1 八時 _____2 シャ ワー _____3 あびます。

4. としょかん _____1 何 _____2 読みますか。

5. バス _____ のりましょう。

6. きのう _____1、大学 _____2 ともだ ち _____3 会いました。

7. にく ＿＿＿＿＿＿＿＿＿＿＿＿＿＿＿＿ 好きですか。

8. 週まつは、九時 ＿＿＿＿＿＿＿＿＿＿＿＿ 1 うち ＿＿＿＿＿＿＿＿＿＿＿＿＿ 2 出ます。

9. 日曜日 ＿＿＿＿＿＿＿＿＿＿＿＿ 1 せんたく ＿＿＿＿＿＿＿＿＿＿＿＿＿ 2 します。

10. 明日 ＿＿＿＿＿＿＿＿＿＿＿＿ 1 かいもの ＿＿＿＿＿＿＿＿＿＿＿＿＿ 2 行きましょう。

11. えき ＿＿＿＿＿＿＿＿＿＿＿＿ 1 前 ＿＿＿＿＿＿＿＿＿＿ 2 ぎんこう
＿＿＿＿＿＿＿＿＿＿＿＿ 3 あります。

12. 毎日 ＿＿＿＿＿＿＿＿＿＿＿＿ 1 おふろ ＿＿＿＿＿＿＿＿＿＿＿＿＿ 2 入りますか。

13. 十時 ＿＿＿＿＿＿＿＿＿＿＿＿ 1 でんしゃ ＿＿＿＿＿＿＿＿＿＿＿＿＿ 2 のります。

14. 先生は　何時 ＿＿＿＿＿＿＿＿＿＿＿＿ 1 うち ＿＿＿＿＿＿＿＿＿＿＿＿＿ 2 かえりました
か。

15. がっこう ＿＿＿＿＿＿＿＿＿＿＿＿＿＿＿＿ はたらきます。

16. うち ＿＿＿＿＿＿＿＿＿＿＿＿ 1 テレビ ＿＿＿＿＿＿＿＿＿＿＿＿＿ 2 見ましょう。

17. うち ＿＿＿＿＿＿＿＿＿＿＿＿ 1 がっこう ＿＿＿＿＿＿＿＿＿＿＿＿＿ 2 でんしゃ
＿＿＿＿＿＿＿＿＿＿＿＿ 3 十分です。

18. わたし ＿＿＿＿＿＿＿＿＿＿＿＿ 1 でんわばんごう ＿＿＿＿＿＿＿＿＿＿＿＿＿ 2
342 ＿＿＿＿＿＿＿＿＿＿＿＿ 3 6801です。

19. わたしは、えい語を話します。日本語 ＿＿＿＿＿＿＿＿＿＿＿＿＿＿＿＿ 話します。

20. かばん ＿＿＿＿＿＿＿＿＿＿＿＿ 1 中 ＿＿＿＿＿＿＿＿＿＿ 2 本
＿＿＿＿＿＿＿＿＿＿＿＿ 3 ノート ＿＿＿＿＿＿＿＿＿＿＿＿＿ 4 あります。

21. カワムラさん ＿＿＿＿＿＿＿＿＿＿＿＿ 1 こうえん ＿＿＿＿＿＿＿＿＿＿＿＿＿ 2 さんぽし
ました。

22. コンピュータ ＿＿＿＿＿＿＿＿＿＿＿＿ 1 てがみ ＿＿＿＿＿＿＿＿＿＿＿＿＿ 2 かきます。

23. さかな ＿＿＿＿＿＿＿＿＿＿＿＿＿＿＿＿ きらいですか。

24. へいじつは日本語のクラス ＿＿＿＿＿＿＿＿＿＿＿＿＿＿ 1 あります
＿＿＿＿＿＿＿＿＿＿＿＿ 2　週まつはありません。

25. びょういん ＿＿＿＿＿＿＿＿＿＿＿＿ 1 どこ ＿＿＿＿＿＿＿＿＿＿＿＿＿ 2 ありますか。

C. Fill in the blanks with either くらい or ごろ, whichever is appropriate.

1. 三時 ＿＿＿＿＿＿＿＿＿＿＿＿＿＿＿＿ おちゃを飲みましょう。

2. うちから大学まで、くるまで一時間 ＿＿＿＿＿＿＿＿＿＿＿＿＿＿＿＿ です。

3. クラスに学生が十人 ＿＿＿＿＿＿＿＿＿＿＿＿＿＿＿＿ います。

4. スパゲッティは890えん ＿＿＿＿＿＿＿＿＿＿＿＿＿＿＿＿ です。

5. 12時半 ＿＿＿＿＿＿＿＿＿＿＿＿＿＿＿＿ にねました。

6. オレンジを十 ＿＿＿＿＿＿＿＿＿＿＿＿＿＿＿＿ 食べました。

D. What suggestions would you make if the person you were with made the following comments? Choose an appropriate response for each comment from among the options below. Not all the responses will be used.

1. _____ おなかがすきましたね。
2. _____ のどがかわきましたね。
3. _____ わたしは、今日はひまです。
4. _____ 明日は日曜日ですね。
5. _____ あさっては日本語のしけんです。
6. _____ つかれましたね。
7. _____ このレストランはおいしいですよ。
8. _____ このえいがはあたらしいですね。

a. じゃ、いっしょに見ましょう。
b. じゃ、ジュースを飲みましょう。
c. じゃ、明日、いっしょにゴルフをしましょう。
d. じゃ、このレストランに入りましょう。
e. じゃ、りょうりしましょう。
f. じゃ、さけを飲みましょう。
g. じゃ、今日の午後、かいものに行きましょう。
h. じゃ、ともだちにでんわをしましょう。
i. じゃ、いっしょにべんきょうしましょう。
j. じゃ、しごとをしましょう。
k. じゃ、休みましょう。

E. A classmate of yours is inviting you to do the following. Decide whether you want to accept or not and give an appropriate response.

1. こんばんディスコへ行きませんか。 _____

_____

2. 今週の金曜日にえいがに行きませんか。 _____

_____

3. 明日の朝五時からいっしょにジョギングをしませんか。 _____

_____

4. 明日の午後、いっしょに日本語をべんきょうしませんか。 _____

_____

5. じゃあ、いっしょにマクドナルドへ行きましょう。 _____

_____

6. ねむい (sleepy) んですか。じゃあ、コーヒーを飲みましょう。 _____

F. Make suggestions in Japanese in response to the following situations.

1. Your friend says that she's hungry but doesn't want to eat alone.

_____

2. Your friend is bored and is looking for something interesting to do.

_____

3. A classmate has fallen behind in Japanese class, and he complains that he doesn't know what is going on.

_____

4. A friend tells you that she doesn't think she should walk home from the library alone at midnight.

_____

G. The non-past, plain, negative forms of all the verbs listed can be found in the array of syllables. Find them and circle them. They may be written top to bottom, left to right, or diagonally starting from the top.

は と か さ な い き て つ あ
た い え そ ら な い か し び
ら あ ら わ な い れ け な な
か れ な な や い ゆ な き い
な た い な い す ね ま な ぬ
い み べ ふ は の き が な も
の が ほ な の い お き え み
ら か さ ま い が き な い な
な な な ぬ が な な て ま な
い い い か な い よ ま な い

きく	おきる	でかける
でる	はいる	はたらく
かえる	いる	あらう
とかす	あびる	たべる
ねる	のむ	つかれる
いく	のる	きがえる
する	みがく	そる
よむ	ぬぐ	みる
きる	はなす	やすむ
		ほす

H. Ask a classmate the following questions in Japanese. Then write down both your question and your classmate's answer.

EXAMPLE: what he bought yesterday.

　　YOU: きのう何をかいましたか。
　　CLASSMATE: あたらしいノートをかいました。

1. what s/he is going to wear tomorrow.

　　YOU: _____ 1

　　CLASSMATE: _____ 2

2. what time s/he left home today.

　　YOU: _____ 1

　　CLASSMATE: _____ 2

3. what time s/he ate breakfast this morning.

　　YOU: _____ 1

　　CLASSMATE: _____ 2

4. where her/his Japanese textbook is.

　　YOU: _____ 1

　　CLASSMATE: _____ 2

5. where s/he is planning to go next Saturday.

　　YOU: _____ 1

　　CLASSMATE: _____ 2

6. where s/he eats lunch every day.

　　YOU: _____ 1

　　CLASSMATE: _____ 2

7. by what means of transportation s/he comes to campus.

    YOU: _____ 1

    CLASSMATE: _____ 2

8. from what time to what time s/he studied Japanese yesterday.

    YOU: _____ 1

    CLASSMATE: _____ 2

9. if s/he likes ice cream, too. (The assumption is that you like ice cream.)

    YOU: _____ 1

    CLASSMATE: _____ 2

10. if s/he likes both *sushi* and *sashimi*.

    YOU: _____ 1

    CLASSMATE: _____ 2

11. with whom s/he ate dinner last night.

    YOU: _____ 1

    CLASSMATE: _____ 2

REVIEW CHAPTER **1**

Listening Comprehension Activities

A. Listen to the following three advertisements for apartments, and decide whether you would like each one or not. Explain the reasons for your opinion in English.

Apt. 1   YES   NO   REASONS _____

Apt. 2   YES   NO   REASONS _____

Apt. 3   YES   NO   REASONS _____

B. Listen to the following four descriptions and identify the kind of place that is being described. Write your answers in the blanks.

USEFUL VOCABULARY

き	tree
いけ	pond
ベンチ	bench

1. _____

2. _____

3. _____

4. _____

C. Listen to this radio commercial for a resort hotel, and circle the answers that best complete the following sentences.

USEFUL VOCABULARY

かんこう	tourism
かんこうきゃく	tourist
れきしてき（な）	historical
じゅうぎょういん	employee
くうこう	airport
すばらしい	wonderful

1. Green Apple Hotel is very special because it is the _____ hotel in the town.
   a. biggest   b. oldest   c. most quiet

2. The hotel has _____ rooms.
   a. 2000   b. 1880   c. 1200

3. It has five _____.
   a. swimming pools   b. coffee shops   c. restaurants

4. The _____ is/are in the basement.
   a. coffee shops   b. restaurants   c. gift shop

5. The hotel's garden is very special because _____.
   a. it is beautiful with many trees   b. there are concerts at night   c. both a and b

6. The hotel is very convenient for foreigners because _____.
   a. the hotel employees speak three different languages
   b. there are many tourists from all over the world
   c. they can enjoy romantic evenings there

7. The hotel is located _____.
   a. next to the airport
   b. in the busiest section of the town
   c. in a very quiet part of the town

D. Listen to the dialogue between Kunio Satoo and Midori Momoi and choose the option that best completes each of the following sentences.

1. Last Saturday was ____ birthday.
   a. Momoi's   b. Momoi's roommate's   c. both a and b

2. She has ____ roommate(s).
   a. one   b. more than one   c. Japanese

3. ____ went shopping on Friday.
   a. Momoi   b. Park   c. Park's roommates

4. Park likes ____.
   a. records   b. music   c. shopping

5. Momoi and her roommates celebrated the birthday ____.
   a. alone   b. with their families   c. with more friends

6. Momoi ____ how to make sushi.
   a. knows   b. is learning   c. doesn't know

7. Satoo ____ eats Chinese and Korean food.
   a. only   b. also   c. never

8. Satoo likes ____ best.
   a. Chinese food   b. Korean food   c. sushi

9. Momoi ____ make sushi again for Satoo's birthday.
   a. wants to and will   b. wants to but can't   c. wouldn't

10. Momoi will be in Japan for a couple of ____ this summer.
    a. days   b. weeks   c. months

11. Satoo's birthday is in ____.
    a. June   b. July   c. August

E. Listen as Satoo and Kraus discuss their long weekend, and then complete the following English summary.

USEFUL VOCABULARY

もう　　　　　*already*
レポート　　　*paper (report)*
…ので　　　　*because, since*

Satoo and Kraus have a long weekend of _____ days. They want to do something

interesting, but they will not go to the Grand Canyon because _____. They won't

go to Disneyland, either, because _____. Satoo suggests that they go to the beach

because it is _____, but they won't go there, since _____.

They won't invite Midori Momoi because she _____. They thought about calling

Ryan Scott because he _____, but they didn't, because he is

_____. In the end, they decide to _____.

KANJI EXERCISES

1. Circle the correct kanji for each of the following meanings.

　1. year　　　　（年）　生

　2. like　　　　学　　（好）

　3. between　　（間）　聞

　4. person　　　入　　（人）

　5. read　　　（読）　話

　6. small　　　（小）　大

　7. right　　　左　　（右）

　8. noon　　　牛　　（午）

　9. rest　　　（休）　体

10. mouth 回 (口)

11. day (日) 月

12. what (何) 向

13. every 母 (毎)

14. name 夕 (名)

15. book (本) 木

16. nine (九) 丸

17. now (今) 会

18. morning (朝) 昼

19. hundred 白 (百)

20. direction (方) 万

21. half (半) 羊

22. ten (十) 千

23. eight 六 (八)

24. top (上) 下

25. town 田 (町)

26. see (見) 貝

27. come (来) 行

28. eat 飲 (食)

29. enter (入) 出

30. seven セ (七)

31. near 遠 (近)

32. gold/money (金) 全

2. Fill in the blanks with the kanji for the words or phrases that are spelled out in hiragana below the lines.

1. きょうしつの _____ 1 に _____ 2 が _____ 3 います。
                         なか   がくせい   ふたり

2. _____ 1 レストランへ _____ 2 きましょう。
   あした   い

3. _____ 1 オレンジジュースを _____ 2 みます。
   まいあさ   の

4. 「お _____ 1 は？」
      なまえ

  「_____ 2 です。」
    やまだ

5. _____ 1 に _____ 2 きました。
  しちじごじゅっぷん   お

6. _____1、わたしはミシガン _____2 の _____3 です。
       いま   だいがく   よねんせい

7. つくえの _____1 にかばんがあります。
       うえ

  かばんの _____2 に _____3 があります。
         なか   ほん

8. _____1 ともだちとでんわで _____2 しました。
   ゆうがた   はな

9. _____1 の _____2 あにと _____3 かけます。
   きょう   ごご   て

10. _____1 の _____2 スミスさんがうちへ _____3 ます。
   らいしゅう   にちようび   き

11. _____ まれですか。
  なんがつう

12. チンさんはちゅうごく _____1 です。_____2 です。
             じん   せんせい

13. わたしはスポーツが _____ きです。
          だいす

14. _____1 の _____2 は一おく _____3 ぐらいです。
   にほん   じんこう   にせんにひゃくまんにん

15. _____1 おふろに _____2 ります。
   まいにち   はい

16. その _____1 は、くるまで _____2 かかります。
     まち   にじかんはん

17. ラジオはよく _____1 きますが、テレビは _____2 ません。
         き   み

18. _____1 に _____2、_____3 レストランで _____4 ごはんを
  いっしゅうかん   に   さんかい   ひる

_____5 べます。
 た

19. _____1 みの _____2 に _____3 を _____4 みます。
  やす   ひ   ほん   よ

20. よく きっさてんへ _____1 きます。そして、コーヒーを _____2 みます。
              い   の

21. いすの _____1 に _____2 さいいぬがいます。
     した   ちい

22. _____1 は _____2 で _____3 べましょう。
  きょう   そと   た

23. _____1 さんの _____2 の _____3 はだれですか。
  やまだ   ひだり   ひと

24. きのう _____1 な _____2 に _____3 いました。
      ゆうめい   ひと   あ

25. えきとぎんこうの＿＿＿＿＿＿＿1に＿＿＿＿＿＿＿＿2きなスーパーがあります。
　　　　　　　　　　　あいだ　　　　　　　　おお

26.「＿＿＿＿＿＿1に＿＿＿＿＿＿2いですか。」
　　　だいがく　　　　　ちか

　　「いいえ、ちょっと＿＿＿＿＿＿3いです。」
　　　　　　　　　　　とお

27.＿＿＿＿＿＿1を＿＿＿＿＿＿2しますか。
　　にほんご　　　　はな

Writing Activities

A. Complete the sentences, telling what people do in each of the following places.

1. としょかんで、_____

2. 大学で、_____

3. レストランで、_____

4. ランゲージラボで、_____

5. えいがかんで、_____

6. デパートで、_____

7. きょうしつで、_____

8. うちで、_____

B. Fill in each blank with a katakana or length mark to create a complete word.

1. シャ _____ ー (shower)

2. _____ ール (beer)

3. レ _____ ード (record)

4. ステー _____ (steak)

5. ア _____ リカ (America)

6. テレ _____ (TV)

7. フ _____ ンス (France)

8. _____ ート (notebook)

9. _____ ーティー (party)

10. ピ _____ (pizza)

11. コ _____ ヒー (coffee)

12. _____ ーダ (soda)

13. タク _____ ー (taxi)

14. _____ ラダ (salad)

15. _____ ラス (class)

C. Fill in each blank with a hiragana to make a phrase. Write *X* if nothing is necessary.

EXAMPLE: 田中さんのアパート

1. わたし _____ でんわばんごう

2. おいしい _____ バナナ

3. おもしろい _____ 本

4. 有名 _____ がっこう

5. やすい _____ くるま

6. 日本 _____ おちゃ

7. きれい _____ うち

8. べんり _____ かばん

9. チンさん _____ ともだち

10. 好き _____ やさい

11. きらい _____ スポーツ

D. Fill in the blanks with particles, paying close attention to the overall meaning of each sentence. Write *X* if nothing is necessary.

わたし _____ ボストン大学 _____ 学生です。きょねん _____、日本 _____ 来ました。とうきょう _____ 日本語 _____ べんきょうしています。

きのう _____、わたしは 日本語 _____ クラス _____ ともだち _____ いっしょに、日本りょうり _____ レストラン _____ 行きました。レストランは ちかてつ _____ えき _____ 前 _____ あります。しずか _____ レストランです。大きい _____、しろい _____ ビルです。

レストラン _____、すきやき _____ すし _____ 食べました。ともだち _____ すきやき _____ すし _____ 食べました。わたしは はし _____ すし _____ 食べました _____、ともだち _____ て (hand) _____ 食べました。

レストラン _____ 先生 _____ 会いました。先生は日本 _____ ビール _____ 飲みました。わたし _____ ビール _____ あまり好きではありません。おちゃ _____ 好きです。

九時 _____ レストラン _____ 出ました。レストラン _____ うち _____ でんしゃ _____ かえりました。十時 _____ うち _____ かえりました。それから、十時 _____ 十一時 _____ テレビ _____ 見ました。十一時 _____ ねました。

E. Write questions for which the following sentences could be the answers. It may be possible to make up more than one question for some of the items.

1. _____
   おんがくを聞きます。

2. _____
   先生がいます。

3. _____
   おもしろいです。

4. _____
   十時にねます。

5. _____
   来月行きます。

6. _____
   きっさてんに行きました。

7. _____
   うちでべんきょうします。

8. _____
   ぎんこうの前にあります。

9. _____
   九つ食べました。

10. _____
    一本かいましょう。

11. _____
    十分です。

12. _____
    4かいです。

13. _____
    四月九日です。

14. _____

今九時十五分です。

15. _____

バスで行きます。

16. _____

28さいです。

17. _____

3000えんです。

18. _____

とうきょうのしゅっしんです。

19. _____

よこい先生のうちです。

20. _____

せんこうはぶん学です。

21. _____

れきしの本です。

I. Someone is interviewing you in Japanese. Answer the questions based on your actual situation.

1. お名前は何ですか。 _____

2. おしごとは何ですか。 _____

3. 何さいですか。 _____

4. しゅっしんはどこですか。 _____

5. どこの大学の学生ですか。 _____

6. せんこうは何ですか。 _____

7. 日本語のクラスは毎日ありますか。 _____

8. 日本語のクラスは何時からですか。 _____

9. 日本語のクラスに学生が何人いますか。 _____

10. おとこの学生は何人ですか。おんなの学生は何人ですか。 _____

11. 大学からうちまで近いですか。 _____

12. あなたのうちのそばにどんなみせがありますか。 _____

13. たいてい何で大学へ行きますか。 _____

14. 何分ぐらいかかりますか。 _____

15. 何時に起きますか。 _____

16. 何時にねますか。 _____

17. 週まつもおなじ (same) ですか。 _____

18. 夕食は何時ごろ食べますか。 _____

19. おたんじょう日は何月何日ですか。 _____

20. きのうクラスへ行きましたか。 _____

21. 先週の週まつには何をしましたか。 _____

22. どんな食べものが好きですか。 _____

About the Authors

Sachiko Fuji was the coordinator of the Japanese language program in the Department of East Asian Languages and Literature, University of California, Irvine during 1991–1992. Before then, she taught Japanese and Spanish for several years at the same campus. She received her M.A. in Spanish literature from Michigan State University, and her Ph.D. in Latin American literature from University of California, Irvine. She is currently teaching Spanish and Latin American civilizations at Japanese universities.

Hifumi Ito has been a lecturer in Japanese at the Program in Japanese Studies, University of California, San Diego since 1989. Currently, she is coordinating the first-year Japanese language course and is in charge of Japanese TA supervision and training. She received her M.A. in Japanese from the University of Minnesota.

Hiroko Kataoka is Associate Professor of Japanese and the Co-director of the Japanese Language Program in the Department of East Asian Languages and Literatures at the University of Oregon. In addition to the Japanese language, she has been teaching Japanese language pedagogy courses. She received her Ph.D. in Education at the University of Illinois, Urbana-Champaign. She has written numerous books, articles, and conference reports on teaching Japanese. She has also given a number of workshops on language pedagogy.

Yumiko Shiotani teaches Japanese as a lecturer in the Department of East Asian Languages and Literatures at the University of Oregon. She also taught at the University of California, San Diego and Berkeley campuses. She received her M.A. in linguistics from the University of Southern California in 1993. She wrote Japanese language learning books and video materials for teachers of Japanese.

Yasu-Hiko Tohsaku is Associate Professor at the University of California, San Diego, where he is the Director of the Language Program at the Graduate School of International Relations and Pacific Studies and the Coordinator of the Undergraduate Japanese Language Program. He received his Ph.D. in linguistics from the University of California, San Diego. He is the author or numerous papers on second language acquisition and Japanese language pedagogy. He is also the author of the main text of *Yookoso!*.